DATE DUE

~~MY 30 96~~			
DE 5 '96			
~~MY 30 96~~			

Demco, Inc. 38-293

Book
design &
production
for the small publisher

Book design & production
for the small publisher

MALCOLM E. BARKER

 Londonborn Publications
San Francisco 1990

First printed June 1990

10 9 8 7 6 5 4 3 2

Manufactured in the United States of America

Library of Congress Cataloging-in-Publication Data
Barker, Malcolm E., 1933-
Book design & production for the small publisher / by Malcolm E. Barker
p.   cm.
Includes bibliographical references.
ISBN 0-930235-08-8 (alk. paper)
1. Book design. 2. Little presses. 3. Book industries and trade.
4. Publishers and publishing.   I. Title.   II. Title: Book design and
production for the small publisher.
Z116.A3B29 1990   90-5460
686--dc20   CIP

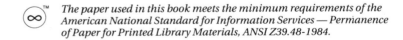

The paper used in this book meets the minimum requirements of the
American National Standard for Information Services — Permanence
of Paper for Printed Library Materials, ANSI Z39.48-1984.

LONDONBORN PUBLICATIONS
370 Fourth Street, P.O. Box 77246
San Francisco, California 94107-7246

Dedicated to the memory of DON GREAME KELLEY who,
with SUSAN ACKER, taught me how to set type by hand at
The Feathered Serpent Press in San Rafael, California.
Thus began my love of typography!

Acknowledgments

Writing a book is usually a one-person task, but producing it requires a sharing of talents by several people. At least that was the case with this book, and there are certain people I particularly want to thank.

Primarily, I thank JACKIE PELS. Not only do I value her expertise as an editor but — more importantly — I cherish her support as a friend.

I am grateful to DAVID R. JOHNSON for his painstaking attention to detail in creating the numerous drawings that are so essential to this book; also, for the meticulous manner in which he pasted up the boards.

I doubt I could have survived my early struggle with the Xerox Ventura Publisher had it not been for the guidance of fellow publisher PETER BROWNING of Great West Books, who never balked at my (seemingly endless) phone calls with computer-related questions.

I am endebted to WALTER SWARTHOUT for his constant encouragement and enthusiasm, and for allowing me the time and facilities to finish the book.

At Adobe Systems Incorporated, GAIL BLUMBERG made it possible for me to work with Utopia typeface while it was still in the testing stage, and DAN KLETTER provided technical support that proved invaluable.

DON GREAME KELLEY and SUSAN ACKER (Feathered Serpent Press, San Rafael) introduced me to the joy of setting type by hand, and I shall be forever grateful to them for that. I dedicate this book to Don's memory.

I owe a special note of gratitude to the small publishers who have sought my guidance during the past five years. Their questions inspired much of this book.

M.E.B.

Credits

I thank the following for permission to use quotations from their publications:
Alfred A. Knopf, *Modern Book Collecting* by Robert A. Wilson; Association of American University Presses, 1986 Book Show catalog; Book Industry Study Group Inc., *Machine-Readable Coding Guidelines;* Frank J. Romano, *The TypEncyclopedia;* ISBN *Users' Manual;* Printing Industries of Northern California, *Printing Trade Customs;* Thomson-Shore, Inc., *Printer's Ink*

The passage by William Safire on page 13:115 is copyright © 1985 by The New York Times Company. Reprinted by permission.

The Haberule is reproduced in Chapter 6 with the permission of Arthur Brown & Bro. Inc., of Maspeth, N.Y.

Appearing as type examples are various passages from *Alice's Adventures in Wonderland* by Lewis Carroll.

Thanks also to the following publishers for allowing me to use their books in illustrating various design elements:
Bicycle Books, *Major Taylor* by Andrew Ritchie (designer, Rob Van der Plas);
Foghorn Press, *Pacific Northwest Camping* by Tom Stienstra (designer, David Morgan);
Great West Books, *The Last Wilderness* by Peter Browning (designers, Peter Browning and Larry Van Dyke); *John Muir In His Own Words* by Peter Browning (designers, Peter Browning and Larry Van Dyke);
Hardscratch Press, *Survival on Montague Island* by Ralph Soberg (designers, David R. Johnson and Jackie Pels);
Heyday Books, *The Earth Manual* by Malcolm Margolin (designer, Sarah Levin); *The Way We Lived* by Malcolm Margolin (designer, Dennis Gallagher);
North Point Press, *Harvest* by Jean Giono; *Notes from a Bottle Found on the Beach at Carmel* by Evan S. Connell; *West of the West,* edited by Leonard Michaels, David Reid, and Raquel Scherr (all books designed by David Bullen);
Novato Historical Guild, *Novato Township* by May Rodgers Ungemach (designer, Carol Keena Aregger);
Windham Bay Press, *Alaska's Inside Passage Traveler* by Ellen Searby (designer, Ellen Searby).

Foreword

Experience teaches that design cannot dictate use. A basic tenet is the old business that form follows function. Countless examples of design excellence have evolved in the natural world, where survival dictates structure and form. Beginning design students are often asked to analyze the egg, the leaf, wind patterns, etc., as inspiration for their own design concepts.

In the realm of books as with any designed object, several common values are derived from the specific use to which any given book will be put. To impose one's sense of "style" upon any manuscript without knowledge of the nature of the manuscript's content is a mistake. Adding style that denies or overshadows the book's content is to become at best decorative, and design is definitely not decoration.

With this in mind, the process of design can be undertaken. First, analyze the content of the manuscript. What is in it? How is the material organized? Which parts of the manuscript are to be of greater or lesser importance as the manuscript is translated into typographical and illustrative elements? Added to this set of inquiries must be an understanding of which type fonts work best for the book in question. Of all the areas to be investigated, the selection of the text and display fonts is the most crucial. How does one select the right font for text? This is not as difficult as one might suspect.

Within the thousands of typefaces there are surprisingly few that have survived as good for text use. Why? The criteria seem to be simplicity of design and unity of shapes of characters as they appear in lines, paragraphs, pages, and chapters of a book. Those type designs that draw attention to the beauty and novelty of individual characters at the expense of the overall color of pages, I reject. I do not wish to imply that traditional type designs work better than those more recently evolved. I have used with equal success both new and old serif and sans-serif faces. Success is based partially on the design of the font or fonts *as applied to the nature of the book's use.*

Develop and use your sense of design. Avoid a decorative approach.

Do not be seduced by any technology. Desktop publishing will not make you any more able to design well than will letterpress printing. Both are wonderful, as are the myriad of technologies that lie between. Remember that all these are simply tools to help achieve an end, and that within this use of tools lies the evolving discipline of design.

One rule is to keep page layout simple. Don't go too far. Never confuse the reader. If you create a printed book through which the message is clearly given in a subtle way, the book will be a design success.

Book design is not *seen* as much as it is *felt*. The user must appreciate the book: words, pictures, and text. All of these blend inseparably in the well-conceived and carefully executed work, which in the end is natural in its form.

Malcolm Barker pays careful attention to these and other aspects of book design. In an easy-to-follow format, he guides you through the maze of grids and layouts, point sizes and papers, covers and bindings. First-time designers — and more experienced small publishers as well — will find straightforward, thorough answers to their questions in this book.

Steve Renick

Steve Renick is Art Director for the University of California Press. His book designs have been recognized by many professional organizations including Bookbuilders West, Graphis Magazine, Internationale Buchkunst-Ausstellung (Leipzieg), The American Institute of Graphic Arts, and The Association of American University Presses. He is the owner of Anselm Design, which specializes in book design.

Summary of contents

Table of contents

I

DESIGN

1

What book design is about

Until a few years ago most books were designed and produced by people who had learned their skills in classrooms and had worked upward through the echelons of design studios and publishing houses. The publishing industry required a vast network of technicians, each skilled in a specific job.

Today, because of computer technology, the situation is quite different. Fewer people can produce more books in less time. And, according to aggressive advertising, all you need is a computer on your desk, along with certain programs, and you can become a *desktop publisher* producing books all by yourself.

The sad truth is that many small publishers are rushing into print without taking time to learn the basics that make the difference between a mediocre book and a well-designed one.

Criteria of design

A well-designed book is one that faithfully embodies the theme of the text. The shape and size are appropriate for the topic. The pages are neither cluttered nor overcrowded. The typeface is legible, and it is suitable for long periods of reading — not so black it becomes forbidding nor so light it causes eye strain. Illustrations are crisp and clear because the paper they are printed on has been selected with care. And, most important of all: A well-designed book is one that does not draw attention to its own design.

Design is the medium, not the message, and is not always easy to define. You know instinctively when a book's design is good: There's that certain feeling from just holding it and flipping the pages. You may not be able to say why you like it, but you know you do. That feeling is not happenstance. It springs from the same source as our reaction to the skillful use of basic principles in music, dance, poetry, painting, or any other art form.

In the following pages I explain the basic principles of book design that have been used by traditional publishers for generations. The idea is not to stifle creative innovations, but rather to provide a structure upon which to mold them. Unless you have had enough experience to be familiar with the nuances of page layout, typefaces, etc., you'd be wise to keep your first designs simple. The first step in being creative and imaginative is knowing what you are doing. When you know the rules, you can decide whether and how to break them.

No right or wrong way

One thing to keep in mind is that there is no RIGHT or WRONG way to design a book. There are more and less APPROPRIATE ways, geared to the theme of the book.

The whole concept of book design is very important if you want your book to look PROFESSIONAL. I will not say this is easy to learn, because it isn't, especially if you have not had graphic arts experience. However, there are certain basic principles which, once you understand and apply them properly, can help you avoid the mistakes seen in many books being published now.

Where do you learn these principles?

In any library or art supply store you can find books dealing with design and/or typography, but they are often so technical you need a background in graphic arts or publishing to follow them. Also, they invariably cover everything from letterheads to billboards, with scant mention of book design.

There are plenty of books about computers and desktop publishing. The majority of these deal with producing newsletters, brochures, advertisements, and business documents. The better ones cover essentials such as basic page layouts for books and tell you how to choose and use the right typefaces for your particular publication. Beyond that, however, they say little or nothing about the intricacies of book design and production.

There are numerous books explaining how to become a publisher, with adequate hints on taking care of legal and business aspects, and working with typesetters. Some explain the complexities of marketing. Few devote more than a couple of pages to explaining the hows and whys of design.

Then there are the colleges and universities that offer either single classes or complete certificate courses.

About this book

In this book I try to bring together the gist of these various resources and present the information in a non-intimidating manner.

The publishing industry is like any other in that it has its own language — technical terms that even the novice must know when dealing with, for example, typesetters and printers. When I introduce these terms I print them in italics and then follow up with an explanation. The same terms, and many others, appear in the glossary at the back of this book.

In many instances I include the historical background, not only because it is interesting but because I believe that we are more likely to remember something if we know how it evolved.

I suggest first reading through the book from beginning to end, then again at your own pace using it as a workbook. I have tried to gather into one place all information pertaining to specific aspects but where this is not possible, or where a cross-reference to a related topic is needed, I provide signposts in the form of

➤   *See page ....*

If there is one standard reference book that you will find on the shelves of almost all publishers it is *The Chicago Manual of Style* (published by The University of Chicago Press). I suggest you buy a copy if you do not already have one. I refer to it frequently in this book (sometimes abbreviating its title to *Chicago* — the name by which it is popularly known). All references apply to the 13th edition.

Two other standard reference books are *Bookmaking: The Illustrated Guide to Design & Production* by Marshall Lee, and *The Design of Books* by Adrian Wilson.

The Self-Publishing Manual by Dan Poynter and *The*

Complete Guide to Self-Publishing by Tom and Marilyn Ross deal at great length with the business aspects of self-publishing.

These and other useful and informative books are listed in the bibliography at the back of this book.

A partial list of related courses appears in Appendix B.

The demands of production

However simple or complex your design ideas are, they have to be set in type and printed to become a book. The techniques used by typesetters and printers have inherent demands that you should know about if you want the best possible results from your concepts. Part II of this book deals exclusively with production, although certain aspects are also discussed in earlier chapters when they relate specifically to design.

It is important that you select the right people to do these jobs for you, making sure they have the equipment and the capabilities to carry out your ideas.

➤ *See Chapter 18.*

My sources

My main sources of research have been from within the traditional printing and publishing industries. When I compare this with what I see and read about in the rapidly changing arena of desktop publishing, I suspect that a lot of the former ways are disappearing not because they are outmoded or obsolete but because they were never learned by the people who write today's textbooks. This is not surprising if you consider the phenomenal speed at which computer-generated printing and publishing are advancing, but it is still to be deplored.

These textbooks beget new teachers whose students then beget more textbooks. A lot of very useful information is not passed on to succeeding generations, which is unfortunate because much of it is still relevant and can benefit even the most innovative book.

The following is as true today as it ever was: A good design can help a bad book. A bad design can harm a good book. A good book with a good design cannot fail.

2

The personality of your book

First you have to decide the shape and size of your book. Although you can do anything you want, you should be aware that there are certain shapes and sizes that are considered standard, and if you differ from these you'll have to pay extra for the privilege. Most of the major printers who work with small publishers consider the following dimensions to be standard:

5½" x 8½"   6" x 9"   7" x 10"   8½" x 11"

The measurements refer to the *trim size* — the size of a page after it has been printed and trimmed. The first figure applies to the width (i.e., from left to right) and the second figure applies to the height (from top to bottom). Remember this when sending out your request for estimates because if you reverse them the printer may base the estimate on the horizontal shape, and the quote will be useless.

The shape you select will depend on a number of factors. If you have several photographs or drawings, and you need large pages to display them, you may want to go for one of the larger shapes. If your book is intended to be carried around (say, a hiking guide), a smaller size may be better — it could fit snugly into a pocket. But generally the 6" x 9" format is the most popular. It will fit on most bookshelves without difficulty, and it is also an easy format to hold and read.

In a manual such as this, readers often need to pause momentarily after being given a specific block of information, and they do not want to feel hemmed in by a page solid with text. Generous spacing will allow them moments of assimilation. Also, if readers need to refer to certain points in the material, their search will be easier if the text has adequate subheadings. For these reasons a larger format is more appropriate.

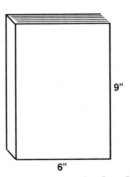

For trim size, the first figure is always the width, and the second is always the height. The upright format is called *portrait*.

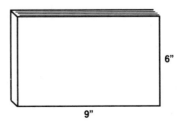

The horizontal format is called *landscape*.

Small picture on 6" x 9" format.

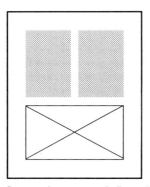

Large picture on 8½" x 11" format.

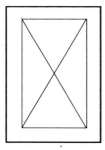

Large picture, sideways on 6" x 9" format.

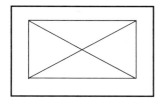

Large picture across landscape format.

You will notice that all of the sizes I listed are vertical formats. What if you want a horizontal shape (known as *landscape*)? Of course you can do it — for a price. Unless they specialize in horizontal formats, most binders set their machines to handle vertical shapes (*portrait*). Consequently, when the occasional horizontal book comes along the machinery has to be realigned, causing delays at the plant — delays which YOU will have to pay for.

For my first book, *Bummer & Lazarus: San Francisco's Famous Dogs*, I chose landscape (8¾" x 5¾") because there were a number of horizontal illustrations that were crucial to the book. If I had used a vertical format my options would have been:

- Print the pictures smaller, so they would fill the width of the page.
- Design a larger format (say, 8½" x 11") so that the pictures could be printed large.
- Print the pictures larger but on their sides.

With the first option I could not give the illustrations the prominence they deserved. The second option would not have been appropriate for such a thin book. And the third was the least desirable of all because of the frustration it can cause a reader when the book must be turned to look at the pictures.

Paperback or hardcover?

Hardcover books are referred to in the industry as either *case bound* (because they are, in essence, bound in a case of stiff boards), or *cloth bound* (because of the material covering the boards). Do not confuse the first term with *slipcase*, which refers to an open-ended box in which one or more books are sold as a unit.

Paperbacks are sometimes called *softcovers*. The separate paper cover on a hardcover book is called a *dust jacket*.

A hardcover edition is more expensive to produce than a paperback one. Although there is a certain prestige to a hardcover book, you need to ask yourself whether people are willing to pay the higher price.

Another consideration should be the anticipated lifespan of your book. Is it a book that will be of interest, or value, to future generations, or is it a manual or instruction book that will be outdated in a few years?

Not so long ago there was a stigma to paperbacks. Except in rare instances, libraries would not buy them, and reviewers would not review them. Bookstores would stock their prime area shelves only with hardcovers. The discrimination could be found also in some homes where people would display hardcover editions in their living room bookcases while relegating the lowly paperback to some less conspicuous location of the house. All that is changing. Although hardcover books still outsell paperbacks, the two are often seen side-by-side on bookshelves and in the review columns.

You can, of course, print both paperback and hardcover. I printed 2,000 paperbacks and 500 hardcovers of *Bummer & Lazarus*, yet the San Francisco Public Library bought fourteen paperbacks. Of all the copies I sold to libraries, only 15% were hardcover.

The actual pages are the same for hardcover and paperback, so the cost up to that point will not be a consideration. What make the big difference are the cover and binding, as discussed in Part II of this book.

How many pages?
You can have any number of pages you want, but again you will pay extra if you go outside certain boundaries.

The pages of a book are printed on large sheets of paper, with either 8 or 16 pages appearing on each side of the sheet. When these sheets are folded they become known as *signatures*, with either 16 or 32 pages now in correct numerical order. The price a printer quotes for printing your book will depend on the number of signatures. All of this is dealt with in greater detail later, but you need to know when planning the shape of your book that the final number of pages ideally should be divisible by 16 or by 32.

Binding
When it's time to bind the pages you will have the following options:

- *Smyth sewn* (stitched with cotton)
- *notch bound* (notched, then glued)
- *perfect bound* (glued)
- *saddle stitched* (with wire staples)
- *side stitched* (stapled along the side)
- *comb bound* (with a plastic spine and prongs)
- *spiral bound* (like a school notebook).

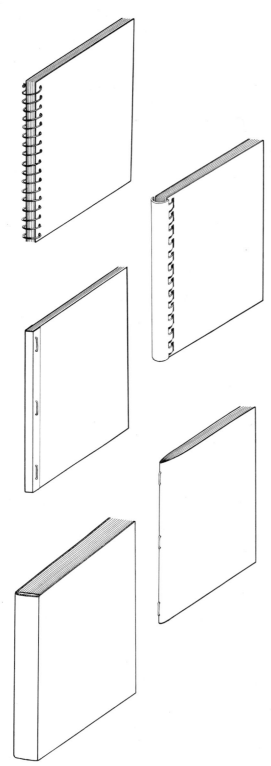

All of these, except the Smyth and perfect bindings, are referred to as *mechanical bindings.*

Spiral bound. The great advantage of spiral binding is that it enables the book to lie flat, and to be folded back to back — both advantageous for cookbooks and manuals. The pages are trimmed on all four sides so that basically you have a stack of single sheets connected with this piece of wire. The process is slightly more expensive than the traditional method, approximately 30 cents to 70 cents more per book than if you have the book perfect bound.

Comb bound. The pages here are also trimmed on all four sides and punched with holes, except that the comb has a solid spine that prevents the pages being folded back to back. If the book is a manual that is likely to be updated this binding enables you to add or remove pages. One advantage of comb binding is that you can print the book's title on it.

Side stitched. These pages are trimmed on all four sides and held together with either strong twine (*side sewn*) or metal staples (*side stitched*) along the side nearest the spine. This method prevents the book from opening flat and also requires a very wide inside margin. It is not appropriate for books thicker than ½".

Saddle stitched. If your book has 64 or fewer pages you should have it saddle stitched because at this size it will be difficult to glue the pages together. The pages are lowered onto a saddle-like device, and two or three metal staples are pressed into the spine. Because the cover is usually attached to the pages during this process the costs are kept to a minimum.

Perfect bound. Today most books are *perfect bound.* That means the cover is glued at the spine after all four edges of the pages have been trimmed. A few years ago, when this method was still in its infancy, the term "perfect binding" seemed a misnomer because pages kept falling out. Now, with vastly improved glues and techniques, this is rarely a problem.

If you intend to publish a book of photographs on enamel coated paper you should stay away from this method because the glue will not adhere to the coating. Even if you insert only one section of coated paper for the photographs, there will always be the chance that those pages could fall out if the book is folded back at the spine.

Notch bound. A good compromise between perfect binding and Smyth sewing is *notch binding.* Only three sides are trimmed, and the fourth is cut diagonally with several notches. Glue is inserted into the notches, to gain a firmer grip on the pages. The cost is less than for Smyth sewing, but more than for perfect binding. Since the pages are not trimmed at the spine you end up with a wider margin.

Smyth sewn. In Smyth (rhymes with "blithe") sewn books the pages are sewn together with thread and then glued to the cover. This is the traditional method, especially for hardcover books, and it costs more per book than the perfect binding method.

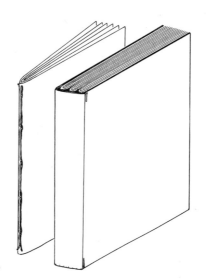

Except in the case of books with coated paper, as mentioned earlier, rarely are paperback books Smyth sewn these days. However, it does add a touch of elegance to a paperback and greatly enhances its durability, so you may want to consider it as an option, particularly if your book is one of lasting value.

A cost comparison

Thomson-Shore, Inc., a major short-run printing company, publishes a quarterly newsletter, *Printer's Ink.* In the Fall 1988 issue they printed the following comparative costs for binding 1,000 copies of a standard 6" x 9" book.

Spiral bound:	$960
Comb bound:	$1,000
Perfect bound:	$400
Smyth sewn paperback:	$715
Smyth sewn hardcover:	$1,580

Remember, these costs are the binding costs only and will be added to other production costs such as paper, set-up, and printing.

Design: the personality of your book

It may help to think of design as the PERSONALITY of a book — the subconscious emotion that is created by a combination of typeface, type style, choice of paper, chapter arrangement, and page layout. To be effective, all these elements should be completely compatible with each other and with the text; furthermore, they should be so subtle that the reader is not consciously aware of them.

One of your first lessons in book design should be a visit to a bookstore. But instead of browsing through the contents of books, concentrate on their design.

- Notice the various shapes and thicknesses.
- Feel the paper they are printed on.
- Look carefully at the way the text is positioned on the pages.
- Is the type easy to read? Can you read it without stumbling over words packed too closely together, or spread too far apart?
- Are the photographs big enough, and cropped properly?
- If a book has a table of contents are the directions clear and concise?
- Does the cover really entice you to pick up the book?
- Does the book FEEL appropriate for its subject matter?
- As you flip the pages do you sense a uniformity of design throughout, or do the blocks of text jump around haphazardly like comic characters dancing across the pages of a child's flip book?
- Do you want to take it immediately to the cash register, or do you want just to drop it without a further thought?

You could supplement this lesson by visiting a library, or a good second-hand bookstore where you can look closely at some older books. You'll find that, although book design has undergone radical changes in recent years, there are still a lot of lessons to be learned from studying books our parents and grandparents enjoyed.

Certain publishers can be relied upon to produce consistently well-designed books. Almost all the books published by Penguin, for example, are excellent models for a standard book of fiction or non-fiction. If you want a good example of more intricate books of illustrations, with exciting page layouts, look at any book published by Time-Life. Look also at books published by university presses.

Even without formal training in graphic design, you will soon begin to sense what works and what doesn't work, once you are familiar with a few basic rules of book design.

While in the bookstore, look for other books written on a topic similar to yours. If yours is a book on baking, look at other cookbooks; if it is a how-to book, look at other self-help books; if it is a travel book check out the travel section. These are the books you will be sharing shelf space with, and you want to be sure yours is every bit as good — or better.

Try to visualize the ideal format for your book. It will help if you can sit quietly where you are completely comfortable, where you feel totally relaxed, almost in a meditative state. If the book is your own, one you have written yourself, you are more likely to have a preconceived notion of how you want it to look.

Be as bold and as imaginative as you can. Do not curb your ideas by thinking "that would be too expensive" or "I could never pull that off." Allow your imagination to reach its limits, and then beyond. Who knows? You might be able to achieve it after all, at a lower cost than you think. But even if you can't, you can work backward from there to a point that is attainable — a point that might still be a long way from your earlier goals.

Look for the theme

What is the theme of the book? Is it an obvious one such as flowers, automobiles, travel, food? Or is it more subtle: love, caring, anger, deceit? Does it concentrate on one particular era in history? Does it try to teach a particular topic or ideal?

When you can answer the question of theme you can begin thinking of a symbol to represent it, an image that can be used somehow in the design to set the mood. A flower. A car. A ship or aircraft. Two people together. Perhaps a strong, heavy piece of artwork with conflicting lines to represent anger. This can be used as a subtle image on the cover, on the title page, on the chapter openers, or integrated with the text.

When you decide on a symbol make sure you find an appropriate rendering of it. If it is a flower, be aware that some flowers carry very distinct impressions. Wild columbine or poppies could imply freedom, a crocus springtime (i.e., an awakening), an hibiscus exotica. Despite what Gertrude Stein said, there is more to a rose than a rose. Depending on its shape and color a rose can conjure up love (red), marriage (white), death (black), or even conflict (a beautiful rose with thorns on its stem). So give careful consideration to your symbol. A bad choice could set a misleading tone to the book and be more damaging than beneficial.

Mood can be expressed not only with selective use of illustrations — line drawing, or photographs — but also with careful use of white space, the arrangement of blocks of text and the placement of headings, as well as the shape of the page, and the texture and color of the paper.

Also, once you have a symbol in mind you may find the creative process taking over, with ideas forming on their own. Jot down the ideas as they come, either in words or quick sketches. If you have the creative ability to write a book you should be familiar with the exhilaration generated as one idea leads to another, and another, until in the end you have something as far removed from your first idea as a computer is from a slate and chalk.

Aim for total harmony
The goal is to produce a book that is in total harmony with what is written on its pages.

My book *Bummer & Lazarus* tells the true story of two stray dogs who lived in San Francisco during the 1860s. Although the obvious symbol was "dogs" I also wanted to say "mid-nineteenth century." On the cover and the title page I used cut-outs of Bummer and Lazarus taken from a contemporary drawing. Because the book consists mainly of the newspaper accounts reporting the dogs' escapades, I printed the text in two columns on each page. To conjure up a sense of the period I set the newspaper mastheads by hand in old metal typefaces which looked as much like the originals as I could find, printed the cover in an old-fashioned sepia color, and selected a warm-tone paper for the pages.

The story is a charming one set in the 1860s. I like to believe that the book is a charming book with an 1860s feel to it.

3

The basics of book design

Generally, as we flip through a book or magazine our gaze falls first on the right-hand page, and then we glance back at the left-hand page. Because of this, the page on the right is considered more important than the one on the left.

A basic rule of book design says that the title page should always be on the right, as should the first page of text. Going beyond that, most designers try to start each chapter on the right, even if they have to leave a blank page facing it. Also, the first page of all elements such as introduction, contents, index, and bibliography should appear on the right. The only exceptions are the copyright page and the frontispiece, both of which go on the left, as is explained later.

In publishers' parlance the right-hand page is called the *recto* (Latin for "right"), and the left-hand page is called the *verso* (Latin for "that which was turned" — in other words, the reverse of the recto). To remember which is which: R for *recto*, R for *right*.

Verso.	Recto.
Latin: that which was turned.	*Latin: right.*

Another basic rule is that the two facing pages are always designed as if they were one page. What happens on the recto should balance, or complement, what happens on the verso. Together, they are referred to as a *double-page spread*, or *spread*.

DICODOB

Another rule is that all elements must work together to create one harmonious effect without any one dominating the others. No matter how beautifully the book is designed, if it does not consistently reflect the theme of the manuscript then it has failed in its duty.

I coined a word to remind myself of this rule whenever

toying with a new idea or concept. Actually, it is an acronym for a question: DICODOB — Does It Complement Overall Design Of Book?

Page layout

The first step is to prepare a layout showing how all the basic double-page spreads will look. Elements to be considered for this are:

- text area
- margins
- *running heads* (those lines of type you often see at the top of each page, above the main text)
- *folios* (page numbers).

Once you decide how these fit on the page you can then deal with those elements that will not appear on all pages, such as *extracts* (quotes too long for inclusion in the text paragraphs), chapter titles, footnotes, and illustrations.

On a large sheet of tracing paper draw the outline of a spread based on the book's trim size, which by now you should have determined. Let's arbitrarily decide your book is 6" x 9", which happens to be the most economical and most widely used format. Rule a carefully measured 12" x 9" rectangle onto your tracing paper. Make this outline bold so it will be easy to read. Then draw a line of dashes down the center, dividing the rectangle into two 6" x 9" pages.

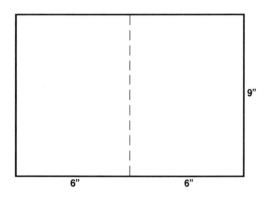

Text area

The shape of the *text area* will depend on the type of book. For a novel and for most non-fiction books, one simple block of text on each page is adequate. For technical books, or manuals like the one you are now studying, the page layout will be more complicated because of different elements such as illustrations and varying degrees of emphasis in the text.

When you add photographs, line drawings, or tables, the total area (excluding margins) becomes known at the *image area*, or *live area*.

A book of photographs requires a page design that allows freedom to vary the positioning and sizing of the photographs while still retaining the basic design. In fact, photo books require even more careful planning

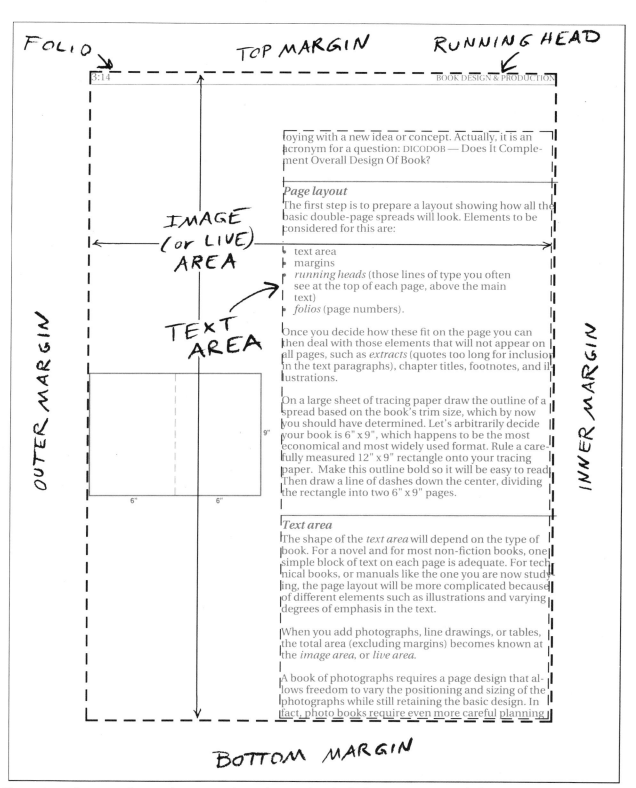

FOLIO

TOP MARGIN

RUNNING HEAD

3:14

BOOK DESIGN & PRODUCTION

IMAGE (or LIVE) AREA

TEXT AREA

OUTER MARGIN

INNER MARGIN

9"

6"   6"

BOTTOM MARGIN

toying with a new idea or concept. Actually, it is an acronym for a question: DICODOB — Does It Complement Overall Design Of Book?

Page layout

The first step is to prepare a layout showing how all the basic double-page spreads will look. Elements to be considered for this are:

- text area
- margins
- *running heads* (those lines of type you often see at the top of each page, above the main text)
- *folios* (page numbers).

Once you decide how these fit on the page you can then deal with those elements that will not appear on all pages, such as *extracts* (quotes too long for inclusion in the text paragraphs), chapter titles, footnotes, and illustrations.

On a large sheet of tracing paper draw the outline of a spread based on the book's trim size, which by now you should have determined. Let's arbitrarily decide your book is 6" x 9", which happens to be the most economical and most widely used format. Rule a carefully measured 12" x 9" rectangle onto your tracing paper. Make this outline bold so it will be easy to read. Then draw a line of dashes down the center, dividing the rectangle into two 6" x 9" pages.

Text area

The shape of the *text area* will depend on the type of book. For a novel and for most non-fiction books, one simple block of text on each page is adequate. For technical books, or manuals like the one you are now studying, the page layout will be more complicated because of different elements such as illustrations and varying degrees of emphasis in the text.

When you add photographs, line drawings, or tables, the total area (excluding margins) becomes known at the *image area*, or *live area*.

A book of photographs requires a page design that allows freedom to vary the positioning and sizing of the photographs while still retaining the basic design. In fact, photo books require even more careful planning

The various elements of a page layout are shown here, using the facing page as an example.

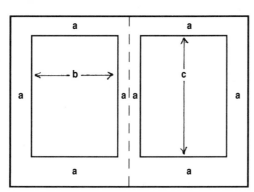

Margins (a) are measured in inches;
text area width (b) is measured in picas;
text area depth (c) is measured
in points, or number of lines.

since each photograph has its own design elements within it, and these have to be compatible with design elements within other pictures on the same spread. Recipe books and books of poetry, for instance, also have unique elements to be considered.

Most of these categories will be dealt with in greater detail when I explain the variety of options you have if you use a system of grids (Chapter 4), but for now let us assume your book falls into the first category — one with a simple block of text on each page.

Typographers have their own way of measuring things. They use *points* to measure individual pieces of type, *picas* to measure the lines of type, or the width of a column, and inches to measure the width of margins. There are 72 points to an inch, and approximately 6 picas to an inch.

Ideally, blocks of text on each page should be the same shape — the same width and the same depth — so that as you flip through the pages you'll see them lined up like guards on parade. The top of one block of text should be in line with the top of the other, and the two bottom lines should be in alignment. If for any reason you cannot have the same number of lines on a page (for example, because of extracts) then let the bottom of the text area go *ragged*. But you should be able to visualize one straight line across the top of the two text areas.

There is a tendency with computer-generated pages to adjust the spaces between the lines and force the two blocks to be the same depth. This is called *vertical alignment*. However, the purist would prefer a ragged bottom to an unevenly spaced page.

Readability tests have shown that the ideal length for a line of type is between 60 and 70 *characters* (letters, numbers, punctuation marks, and spaces between words). This translates into a column approximately 26 picas wide (roughly 4¼").

Margins

Margins provide the white space that is essential to relieve the tension of all that text. Do not fall into the trap of having minuscule margins in order to get as much type on the page as possible to save on costs. The formula *fewer pages = less paper = higher profit* often results in an ugly book.

Usually the width of the margins varies. The margin closest to the binding is narrower than the one on the outer edge of the page, and the top margin is narrower than the one at the bottom of the page. If we had only one page to deal with there would be no confusion when referring to the first two margins as "left" and "right," but it could be misleading when viewing both pages of a spread as one area. That is why designers and typographers use the terms *inner margin* (the one "inside," closer to the binding), and *outer margin* (the one on the outside edge of the spread).

Two more points to keep in mind are:

- Depending on the thickness of your book, a certain amount of the inner margin will disappear into the fold.
- When the pages are trimmed you may lose a fraction of an inch from the outer margin.

These points are not as insignificant as they may seem. If you ignore them in this early planning stage you will wonder why, when the book arrives from the printer, the overall proportions are off, and the inner and outer margins are narrower than you had planned.

Allow at least ⅝" for the inner margin if the book is about 1" thick, and more if the book is thicker. To play it safe, anticipate that at least ¹⁄₁₆" will be trimmed off the outer margin, and plan accordingly.

When you mount a photograph in a frame you leave more room at the bottom than at the top. In placing your text area on a page you will do the same thing, for the same reason: If placed in the exact center it will have the illusion of slipping off the page. When the top and bottom margins are identical the sheer volume of the text area seems to make the bottom margin appear smaller.

The traditional way

In recent years there has been a tendency to leave more space at the top of the page than at the bottom in books larger than 6" x 9", since the upper half is considered the more important portion of a page.

The traditional style (i.e., with a larger margin at the bottom) evolved over several generations and became the standard for most books with one block of text per page. This was based on the principle 1½–2–3–4, which

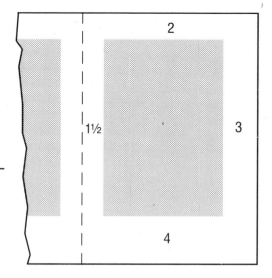

In the traditional 1½-2-3-4 formula, the inner margin (1½) is half the width of the outer margin (3), and the top margin (2) is half the depth of the bottom margin (4).

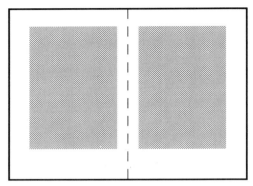

Applying the 1½-2-3-4 formula gives a good balance to a double-page spread.

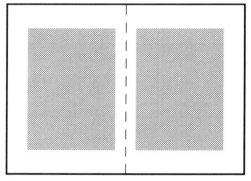

When the top and bottom margins are the same the text looks as if it is falling off the page.

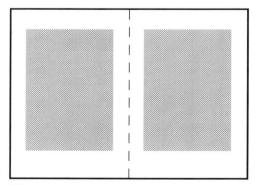

When the outer margins and inner margins are the same, the two inner ones create an extra wide space that can alienate the two blocks of text.

specifies that the inner margin should be half the width of the outer margin and that the top margin should be half the depth of the bottom margin.

Do not be misled by the numbers 1½-2-3-4: They do not refer to inches but to the relative proportions of the margins. Exactly how they translate into inches will depend on the dimensions of your text area and the trim size of your page. Such generous margins would be more suited to larger trim sizes (e.g., 8½" x 11") than they are to the 6" x 9" page.

You can see why the outer and inner margins should not be the same width. On a double-page spread the two inner margins would combine to create a gap twice as wide as the outer margins, thus causing a sense of alienation of the two blocks of text. If the inner margins are only half the size of the outer margins to start with, they will combine to create a more symmetrical pattern. But remember the thickness of your book, and do not make these inner margins too narrow.

Today this traditional format is being challenged by an explosion of new ideas as computer technology generates a mass of home-brewed designs. As in any field, good innovative ideas are needed. Feel free to experiment, but keep in mind you are designing a book, and books should be READER FRIENDLY if they are to invite pleasurable reading.

The small publisher without a background in graphic arts or design is better off staying within the confines of certain time-honored formulas rather than taking the chance of compromising the manuscript.

However, I don't advocate using the 1½-2-3-4 formula for all books. It is suitable for novels and most straightforward non-fiction, but it could be boring for a how-to book, or a book of enticing recipes, or any number of other non-fiction books. If I had employed it for this book I would have been limited in use of illustrations, and you might have had a harder time locating points of immediate interest.

Running heads

Traditionally, the title of a book runs along the top of each left page, and the title of the chapter or section runs along the top of each right page. To distinguish them, each is set in a different font or style — usually small capitals for the book title and italics for the chapter or section title. Merely using slightly different sizes of the same face as the text will not be sufficient to make the necessary distinction, unless, perhaps, you separate the heads from the text with a thin horizontal *rule* (line), or place them in the center where they are less likely to be confused with the first line of text.

These are called *running heads*, or *headers*, and must be designed with care. They appear every time your reader turns a page and so should be subtle enough not to become a distraction. They should be visible when needed but invisible at all other times.

Different books, different headers. The nature of your book will determine how to handle running heads. In a novel it may be sufficient to have the book's title on either one or both of the pages, whereas for non-fiction you could use a section title on the left page and a chapter title on the right one. Some books do not require running heads, if the reader has no need to refer to them: After all, surely readers know the name of the book they are reading without being reminded every time they turn a page.

If the book is a reference work there is a possibility teachers will make multiple copies of certain pages for distribution to their students, in which case everyone benefits when the title is included on each spread (the publisher benefits if the students are thus encouraged to buy the book).

Because running heads normally do not extend across the full width of a page they can be considered part of the upper margin when you calculate the margin sizes. In other words, measure the upper margin from the top of the page to the top of the first line of text and allow the running head to sit approximately two-thirds of the way down.

Sometimes the book's title and the chapter title run along the bottom of a page to create a constant base line for spreads on which the columns of text are not of equal length. Not surprisingly, these are known as *running feet*, or *footers*.

Extra spacing should be left between headers and the body of text. Or you can use thin rules along the full width of the image area to separate these two elements.

For the sake of uniformity, the placement of headers on the page should be consistent with the placement of

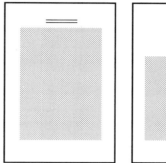

Running heads should be consistent with chapter titles. If one is centered, the other should be centered ...

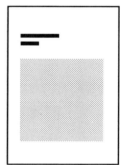

... if one is flush left, the other should be flush left.

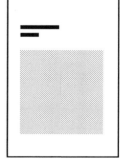

Running heads set flush right on a verso page and flush left on a recto work well when chapters always start on a recto with headings set flush left.

chapter titles or other display type. In other words, if chapter titles are centered, then the headers should be centered; if they are flush left or flush right then the headers should be placed accordingly.

For aesthetic reasons they should not appear on blank pages. Similarly, they can be left off illustrated pages if their presence is disturbing.

In this book I have used a thin horizontal rule on the running heads, partly for design reasons but primarily to define the width of the image area of the page.

Also, as you can see, I have placed the recto header flush left (as is the style with my chapter titles) but have placed the verso header flush right where I feel it complements the overall layout of the two-page spread.

Folios

Just because the page number (the *folio*) is the smallest element on a page does not mean you can place it haphazardly. Its position is very important and will vary with the type of book. Bear in mind that the easiest place to look for a folio is the upper outside corner of a spread (that is, the upper left corner of a verso page and the upper right corner of a recto page). The hardest place to find it is tucked close to the binding.

Keep these points in mind when deciding where to place the folio:

- In reference books the page numbers should be easy to find and clear enough to read while flipping through the pages.
- If a reader is unlikely to refer to a specific page number (as with a novel) the position of the folio is less critical.

In this book I constantly refer to specific chapters. To make it easier for my readers to find them I have placed the chapter number with the folio on each page. The chapter number is set 1 point larger, and is followed by a colon.

Depending on how the running heads are set in type, you might consider placing the folio with them on the same line. In doing this you could either keep the folio within the text area (using a size large enough to be seen easily) or have it extend slightly beyond. However, this may prove more inconvenient (and costly) if the

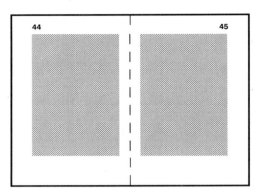

Folios are generally easier to find when placed on the outside of a spread, whether at the top or the bottom of each page.

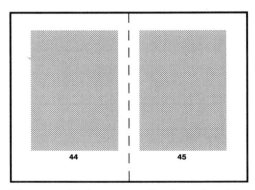

They can also be seen easily when placed in the center of each page, whether at the top or the bottom.

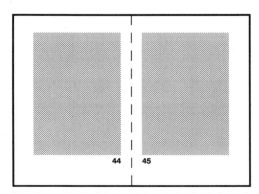

The least desirable position is tucked closed to the binding — top or bottom.

typesetter intends to print each running head only
once and then repeat it for all pages where it appears.
Discuss this with your typesetter. If you are doing the
typesetting yourself with a desktop publishing program
you will need to consider these options.

The question of when not to use page numbers will be
dealt with later in this book.

➤   *See page 9:73.*

Back to the layout

Once you understand the significance of the text area,
margins, running heads, and folios, you can return to
your 12" x 9" tracing and determine a basic layout for
the pages of your book.

Keeping in mind the rule about viewing the two pages
as one unit, you should now make several rough
sketches. These can be done either on sheets of paper
that can be held under the tracing, or, better still, you
can make a series of *thumbnails* (mini-sketches) within
rectangles reduced to approximately one-third of the
original. When preparing for thumbnails, be sure that
the outlines are in exact proportion to the original or
you will not get the correct perspective. For example,
12" x 9" will reduce to 4" x 3".

Two ways of doing this:

- Carefully measure one or more of your
  (4" x 3") mini-outlines on a sheet of paper
  and have several photocopies made.
- Cut the (4" x 3") rectangle from a piece of
  cardboard and use it as a template to trace as
  many outlines as you need. If you nick the
  center of the top and bottom edges you will
  have a guide when drawing the line of dashes
  separating verso and recto pages.

When you find the combination you want, draw an outline of the text area, running head, and folio position
on your tracing paper.

Congratulations! You now have a master guide for all
subsequent pages throughout your book.

The final measurements of the text area cannot be
determined until you have selected the style and size
of type you want for the text, but at least you have a

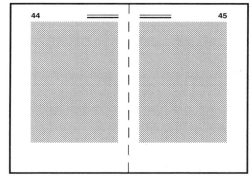

A basic layout for the 6" x 9" format.

good approximation on which you can base those decisions.

The whole question of type is a crucial and complicated one, and I have devoted four chapters to it. But first I want to show you other possible page layouts, using the grid system.

4

Working with a grid

For most books of straight text, the samples used in the previous chapter should be adequate. However, for books larger than 6" x 9", especially if they have illustrations and two or more columns of text, you need the help of a *grid*. This is a system of vertical and horizontal lines used to apply principles of proportion and their relationship to each other in a design layout. It enables you to organize your pages so they have a sense of uniformity. For the novice this may be intimidating, but using the simplest grid can add a professional look even to a first book. Try it — you'll like the results!

The image area
Before you begin thinking about a grid you should have a basic idea of what the book's design will be. You will need to know the size of the page and have a rough idea of how much of the page will be occupied by the *image area* (text and illustrations combined). You should also know what mood you want to create: for example, does the book's topic call for a light, carefree treatment, or a more serious, scholarly approach? Are you dealing only with text, or are there illustrations scattered across the spread? When you have all this firmly in mind you can start to design a grid.

It can be a simple grid of vertical columns defining your text area and the margins that surround it. This alone can be a valuable tool providing you with basic guidelines that will ensure consistency throughout your book.

Or you can add to this a set of horizontal lines that will act as a guide for including illustrations and headings. You can go further and divide the grid so intricately that it will determine just where lines of text will fall, and where to place captions and folios. But beware!

The more complex it is the more likely it will become the master rather than the servant of your design. Keep it simple, and flexible.

In the beginning you will be doing a lot of guesswork, trying different ratios of image area versus overall page area. A good way to start is to determine a suitable width for the image area and deduct it from the overall page width. You can then divide what is left into two margins.

Take the 6" x 9" page as an example. If you want one column of text about 4¼" wide, you deduct the 4¼" from 6". This will leave you a total of 1¾" for the two margins. You could make the inner margin ¾" and the outer margin 1". Use the same principle to figure out the top and bottom margins.

Again, the exact measurements cannot be known until later, when you have decided which size and style of typeface to use, but first you should find a basis upon which to work.

You can run text in one column across the width of a 6" x 9" page, but do not try it with larger pages, except, maybe, in a children's book which has exceptionally large type and generous spacing. Remember that lines longer than 60-70 characters are difficult to read in a continuous text. Two narrow columns are not only easier to read but save space, because the shorter lines can be printed in smaller type with less space between the lines and still be readable.

As stated at the opening of this chapter, a grid is particularly suited to books larger than 6" x 9". The following examples are based on an 8½" x 11" page, and use two basic starting points: Either the image area is 41 picas wide or it is 39 picas wide.

41 picas: 2 columns

We can divide the first image area into two columns, each 20 picas wide, with a 1 pica *gutter* between them.

This may seem simple enough, but it can present pitfalls for the unwary designer. You will have to watch where your headings and subheadings fall.

- If two subheadings appear next to each other in the two columns they create a *tombstone* effect.

- If only one or two words appear at the top of a column they create a *widow*.
- To ensure a well-balanced layout you should not have fewer than three lines at the top of a column before a heading, or fewer than three lines at the bottom following a heading.
- If your text is not *justified* (that is, the lines are not of equal length), it is a good idea to insert a thin *rule* (line) down the gutter to help tidy up the visual effect of the ragged line lengths.

Photographs and other illustrations can be placed across either column or both. This will be dealt with at greater length in Chapter 16.

---

41 picas: 3 columns

We can also divide the same 41-pica area into three equal columns of 13 picas, with 1-pica gutters separating them. Although you are unlikely to set your type in three columns you could set it across two of those columns (including one gutter), and leave the third (and its gutter) as a margin in which to place illustrations, comments, or subheadings. You could, of course, leave the third column blank.

In this combination you would have a text column that is 27 picas wide (2 x 13 + 1 x 1), and a margin that is 14 picas wide (1 x 13 + 1 x 1).

Already you can see exciting possibilities of arrangement, all utilizing the classic ⅓–⅔ formula:

- both text areas on the left side of each page
- both on the right side
- both in the center of the spread
- both on the outer edge of the spread.

The two latter choices are called *mirror images*.

A three-column grid also lets you extend photographs across two columns, with captions in the third column.

At this point you should take into consideration what paper you will be using. If the paper is too thin, or is not opaque, the images on your pages will show through. In this case you should select a layout in which the blocks of text will back onto each other.

➤ *See Chapter 23, which deals with paper in more detail.*

Working with a 41-pica area.

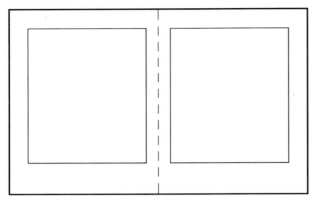

Starting with a basic 41-pica area on each page ...

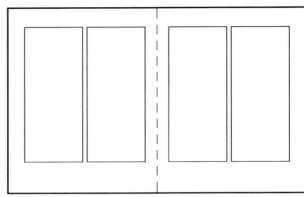

... you can create 2 20-pica columns with 1-pica gutter ...

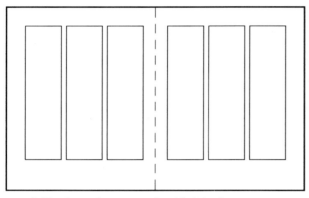

... or 3 13-pica columns, each with 2 1-pica gutters.

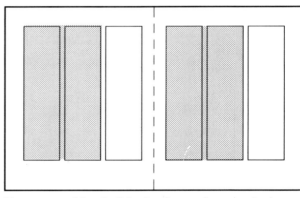

You can combine 2 of the 3 columns for text, placing them either to the left or right on each page ...

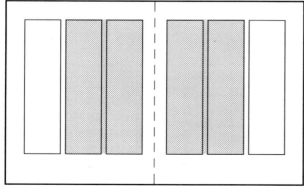

... or in the center of the spread ...

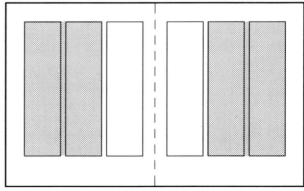

... or on the outer edges of the spread.

Working with a 39-pica area.

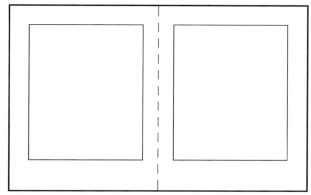

Starting with a basic 39-pica area on each page ...

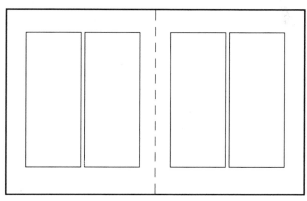

... you can create 2 19-pica columns with 1-pica gutter ...

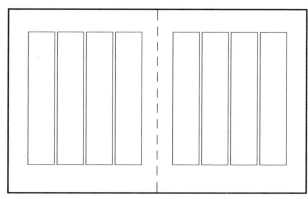

... or 4 9-pica columns with 3 1-pica gutters ...

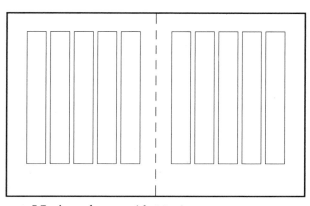

... or 5 7-pica columns with 4 1-pica gutters.

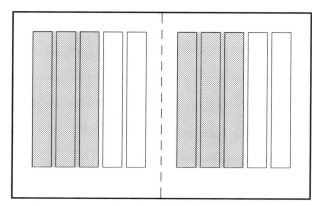

Combine any number of columns for text ...

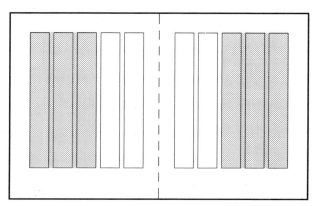

... and find an appropriate placement.

39 picas: 2 columns

Starting out with a width of 39 picas we have a different set of choices.

You can still get two equal columns, each slightly narrower than before (19 picas instead of 20 picas). But to break a 39-pica area into three columns and two gutters you'd be dealing with ⅓ picas, which can get complicated for the novice. However, we can easily get four- and five-column grids from a 39-pica area.

39 picas: 4 and 5 columns

Divide each of the 19-pica columns into two equal 9-pica columns with 1-pica gutters, and you have four columns. Now you can spread your text across either two columns (19 picas), or three columns (29 picas).

You can even divide the 39-pica area into five columns each 7 picas wide, with 1-pica gutters separating them. Again, you would not set type in such narrow columns, but your design choices are broadened by the different ways you can combine them.

Why so many columns?

By now, some readers are probably wondering why they should go through this exercise of multiple columns if they end up with only the one wide column of text and an extra wide margin. The answer is that with careful computation those two blocks are more likely to be in correct proportion to each other on the page, thus creating a more balanced visual effect than if you indiscriminately cordoned off two blocks. Also, if you include photographs you are more likely to place them where they have greater impact on the spread.

This book has five columns

The pages of this book are based on a five-column grid. Within the margins is an image area 39 picas wide (approximately 6½"). This image area is broken into five columns each 7 picas wide, with four 1-pica gutters.

By combining three columns and two gutters I have a 23-pica text area. This leaves me a 1-pica gutter and a 15-pica area in which I can place small illustrations.

I tried several other combinations of column widths but they did not allow the flexibility I needed. A major consideration was that I wanted a single column of text no wider than 24-25 picas. Once I decided on this format I used it as a guide for positioning the headings, subheadings, illustrations, captions, etc. Even the placement of small illustrations on pages such as this one is influenced by the width of that outer column.

The actual grid is reproduced on the front and back covers of the book. Notice how each one of the reduced pages on the front cover occupies one column, while the title stretches across four columns. The lines above and below the two names are not random: they echo the book's three-column text area.

However, the 23-pica text area would not work well with the back matter pages, nor with the table of contents. Returning to the basic grid, I divided the five columns into two blocks of text each equal to 2½ columns and separated them with a gutter. Then, to maintain a thread of familiarity throughout the book, I placed the appendix headings in the same position as the chapter headings. DICODOB lives!

Moral: Let the grid guide you, not box you in.

Horizontal divisions

Unless your book is heavily illustrated, you really do not need to concern yourself with horizontal divisions. The principle is the same as for vertical divisions in that the area is divided into several equally proportioned units. These horizontal units are usually based on the number of lines of text you have on a page, with the spaces that separate them being the thickness of a line of type rather than an arbitrary 1 pica as with vertical divisions.

Start by dividing your page into three equal horizontal divisions. This will come in handy when designing the first page of each chapter because, as I explain later, the text on those pages usually begins approximately one-third from the top. If you have large-size chapter numbers and a title that is several lines long, you could divide that upper one-third unit into three equal units to help you lay out the elements so they maintain a sense of harmony with each another.

My image area is equal to 56 lines of type, and it divides easily into three horizontal units of 18 lines separated by two 1-line gaps. The depth of each line of type is measured to include the type itself as well as the space

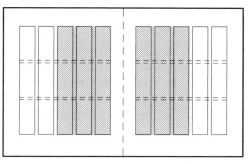

The basic grid of this book is based on a 39-pica area. On each page are 5 7-pica columns and 4 1-pica gutters. The text occupies 3 columns and 2 gutters on each page and is centered on the two-page spread.

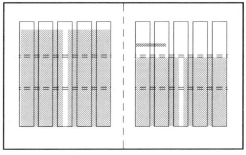

For pages in the back matter the columns are divided into two blocks of text each equal to 2½ columns (19 picas).

beneath it (*leading*). The running head appears at the top of the text area. Then there is a gap, followed by 51 lines of text. On the first page of each chapter there are only 37 lines of text beneath the heading.

For readers who wish to study the grid principle in greater depth I recommend Allen Hurlbert's *The Grid and Layout*, Jan V. White's *Editing by design* and *The Grid Book*, and John Miles' *Design for Desktop Publishing* (all of which are listed in **Recommended reading**, at the back of this book).

➤ *See also Chapter 16, which shows how a grid can help you arrange photographs on your pages.*

5

A type primer

Your most important decisions when designing a book will involve typefaces. Which faces do you use? What sizes should they be? How much spacing between words, and how much between lines? When — and why — do you use italic type, or bold type? How large should the large letters be, and how small the small?

These factors determine not only the physical appearance of your text but also the relative ease with which it can be read. Subliminally, they set the tone and pace for the whole book.

Each typeface has its own personality, and you need to find one that is compatible with the theme of your book. I admit it can be intimidating at first, trying to sort your way through the mass of faces and fonts, picas and points, serifs and sans serifs. But once you understand a few fundamentals of typography and learn to recognize the influence certain characteristics have on reading habits, you will feel less threatened and more stimulated.

What I hope to do in this chapter, and the three following it, is give you a working knowledge of typefaces so you are better able to make up your own mind which to use, and how to position them on your pages.

Five ways with one book
A few years ago, five university presses participated in a project in which each went through the process of editing and designing a book for the same manuscript. The results were published by William Kaufmann Inc. in a book entitled *One Book/Five Ways.*

There are several lessons for the small publisher within the covers of that book. Of particular interest, perhaps, is the fact that no two presses chose the same typeface. They selected Garamond (University of Chicago), Goudy Old Style (University of Texas), Helvetica (University of North Carolina), VIP Sabon (University of Toronto), and Palatino (Massachusetts Institute of Technology).

The topic of the manuscript was house plants. So much for the axiom that there are only "one or two" typefaces for a particular manuscript!

Typefaces

For many years Jenson, Garamond, Caslon, Baskerville, Bookman, and Century were the favored faces for most categories of books. This has changed with the advent of computers and the rapid rise of desktop publishing. A whole new industry has sprung up, with software companies either making subtle changes to those older faces so they can be compatible with the latest printing technology, or designing totally different faces. To get around trademark and copyright laws, manufacturers alter individual letters of established faces and then sell them under new names.

Century is interwoven with Cambridge Expanded, Cambridge Schoolbook, Century Schoolbook, and also Century Modern. Helvetica has provided the genes for Claro, Geneva, Helios, Swiss, and Vega. And Times Roman has spawned Dutch, English, English Times, London Roman, and Times New Roman. These are a few of the confusing signposts the novice designer can expect to encounter.

Almost any of these older faces or their newer incarnations may be suitable for your book. However, be wary of Times. Its slim letters are more appropriate for the narrow columns of a newsletter than they are for the wide text area of a book. On many desktop publishing programs it is the only serif face available, unless you pay extra for other choices, and consequently it is seen almost everywhere. There is a danger it may reach saturation point and become passe.

Much of the terminology used in typography dates back to the days when typesetting was done by hand, using individual pieces of metal type. The hand-set method gave way when machines set type one line at a time from lead which could be recycled immediately after use (called *linotype*). This in turn was superseded by computer-generated type.

Fonts and character sets

It may help to think first about typewriter type, with which most of us are already familiar.

On your typewriter keyboard are 26 letters which you can type as either *uppercase* (capitals) or *lowercase*. You also have numbers 1 through 0, plus an assortment of punctuation marks, fractions, accents, and symbols. This will give you a choice of approximately 100 *characters*. The typographic term for this total assortment is *font* — a word now being threatened by computerese.

Traditionally, a font is a set of characters of a specific size within a typeface. For example, a group of 10-point Baskerville characters is one font, while a group of 12-point Baskerville characters is another font. In the days of hand-set type each font was stored in its own drawer. Today the word is used interchangeably with "typeface," much to the chagrin (and confusion) of typesetters who learned their craft the traditional way. In this book "font" retains its traditional meaning.

Now, when referring specifically to the assortment of characters within a typeface, typesetters use the term *character set*, which does not apply to any particular point size.

Typefaces used for printing also have fonts although they often extend closer to 200 characters, including such less familiar items as *ligatures* (two or more characters designed as one unit, such as fi, ffi), and *small capitals* (a set of capital letters specially designed to be the same height as lowercase letters).

Type sizes

In a typewriter you usually have the choice of *pica* or *elite*. These refer to the width of the actual type. Pica has 10 characters per inch. Elite has 12 characters per inch. Obviously, if any 10 (or 12) characters are to measure 1 inch, then they must all be the same width: an *m* must be the same width as an *i*, for example. The wider characters are squashed and the narrower ones stretched. That is why we say typewriter faces are *monospaced*.

Typefaces used for printing are designed differently. Each character is given *proportional spacing*, allowing the subtleties of each to determine the width.

Alphabet

monospaced

Alphabet

proportional

Picas and points

The word *pica* takes on a different meaning when you are dealing with print typefaces. Here, a pica is a unit of measurement used to determine the length of a line of type, or the width of an area.

One pica measures .166", which means that 6 picas measure slightly less than 1" (.996"). You can round it out to one inch as long as you are dealing with small numbers, but be warned you could cause serious errors when calculating a large number of lines by using the 6 picas = 1" formula.

The size of type is measured in points.

- 12 points = 1 pica
- 6 picas = 1"
- 72 points (12 x 6) = 1".

How type is measured

Each piece of metal type produced in the United States had exactly the same measurement from surface to base — .9186" (referred to as *type-high*) — so that when they were *locked up* (secured on the press for printing) they would leave an even impression on the paper.

On top of each piece of metal sat the individual character (*face*), which became known by the dimensions of the surface upon which it sat. The depth of the surface when measured in points was the typeface's *point size*, and the width of the surface became the face's *set* (or *set-width*).

Lowercase characters are known by their *x-height* (named after the letter *x*), and uppercase letters are known by their *cap-height*.

Type designers varied the sizes of type on the surface of these blocks of metal, labeling them according to the measurements of the surface rather than the size of type as seen on the printed page. For example, all of the letters in this illustration are defined as 16-point, even though some are obviously smaller than others.

Their width (set) varies, with some allowing more characters on a line than others. So you cannot assume that all 10-point type will have the same number of characters per line. Also, the different weights of the body will require different spacing between the lines.

hoe **hoe** hoe **hoe** hoe

Five different typefaces, all 16-point.

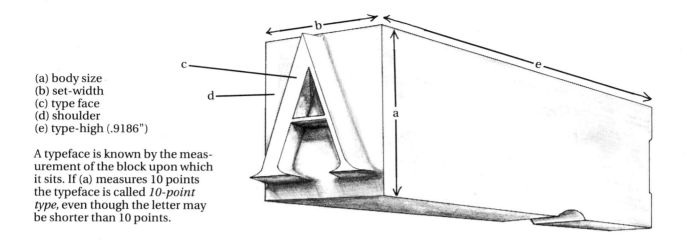

(a) body size
(b) set-width
(c) type face
(d) shoulder
(e) type-high (.9186")

A typeface is known by the measurement of the block upon which it sits. If (a) measures 10 points the typeface is called *10-point type,* even though the letter may be shorter than 10 points.

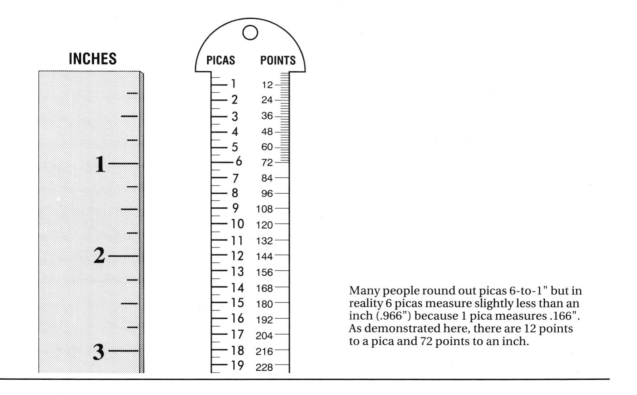

INCHES

PICAS	POINTS
1	12
2	24
3	36
4	48
5	60
6	72
7	84
8	96
9	108
10	120
11	132
12	144
13	156
14	168
15	180
16	192
17	204
18	216
19	228

Many people round out picas 6-to-1" but in reality 6 picas measure slightly less than an inch (.966") because 1 pica measures .166". As demonstrated here, there are 12 points to a pica and 72 points to an inch.

cap-height

x-height

point size

Because of the confusion this can cause, some typographers use the x-height as a more reliable indicator of a face's size since it is more constant than the point system. Other typographers use the cap-height.

Anatomy of a letter

In the same way we respond to certain characteristics on another person's face, so we respond to certain characteristics of a typeface. One person's nose may be wider, narrower, longer, stubbier, more fleshy, or more bony than another person's. The shape of the mouth may be quite different, as may the cheekbone structure. And so it is with type.

The letters of some typefaces have stubby bodies with no variations in the thickness of their stems, while others are more elegant and have graceful stems that fluctuate from thick to thin. Some letters begin and end with delicate little strokes, called *serifs*, while others are abrupt. The stress at narrow parts of individual letters such as *o, e,* and *g* will vary from one face to another.

In some faces certain letters have highly individual characteristics, such as the upraised arms on the uppercase Y of Palatino. The uppercase P of Palatino is also unique in that its bowl has a gap where the arm doesn't quite reach the upright stem.

The cumulative effect is what creates the personality of each typeface. These details may not always be noticed but, combined, they influence how you read the text.

YP
Two very distinctive letters of Palatino.

Sans serif faces

Some typefaces do not have any serifs at all, which is why they are called *sans serif* (*sans* meaning "without" in French). The chief characteristic of sans serif faces is that their letters do not stress, nor (with rare exceptions such as Optima) do they have thick and thin variations to their strokes. The absence of these features helps create a personality unique to sans serif faces.

The total effect created by all these variations will give you the typeface's personality.

The chief characteristic of sans serif faces is that their letters do not stress, nor (with rare exceptions such as Optima) do they have thick and thin variations to their strokes. The absence of these features helps create a personality unique to sans serif faces.

Helvetica, a sans serif face. Compare it with the Utopia used for the main text.

Putting it all together

So much for individual letters. Now let us consider some of the characteristics that become apparent only when a typeface is seen as a complete block of text.

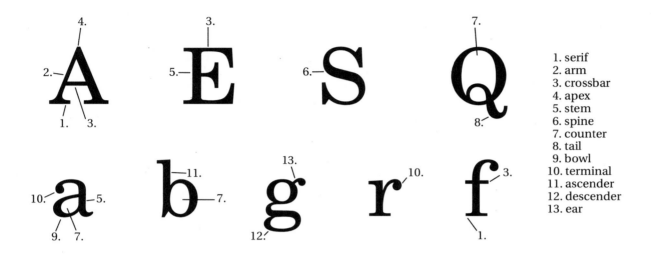

1. serif
2. arm
3. crossbar
4. apex
5. stem
6. spine
7. counter
8. tail
9. bowl
10. terminal
11. ascender
12. descender
13. ear

J J J J J J

g g g g g g

Same letters, same size (all are 48-point). Yet each one has its own personality.

There was a large mushroom growing near her, about the same height as herself; and, when she had looked under it, and on both sides of it, and behind it, it occurred to her that she might as well look and see what was on top of it. She stretched herself up on tiptoe, and peeped over the edge of the mushroom, and her eyes immediately met those of a large blue caterpillar, that was sitting on the top, with its arms folded, quietly smoking a long hookah, and taking not the smallest notice of her or of anything else.

Wide spaces between words in text create rivers of white. This often happens when a thin-bodied typeface is set justified in wide columns and when a broad-bodied typeface is set justified in narrow columns.

The lowercase alphabets of each typeface consist of three main parts: *x-height* (or *body*), *ascenders*, and *descenders*. The ascenders are the loops that extend upward from the body, as in b, d, f, h, k, l, and t. The descenders are the loops that drop down from the body, as in g, j, p, q, and y.

When text is seen in a block all of these elements will meld. The height of the ascenders, the depth of the descenders, and the shape of the body, combined with the spacing added between the lines (*leading*), are what affect your response to the typeface as a whole when you are reading it on a page.

Some faces have very long ascenders and descenders, necessitating additional leading between the lines. In most texts ascenders outnumber descenders, and there is little chance they will touch one another. However, if they do touch they create subconscious stumbling blocks for your reader. You should watch out for this when looking through printed samples of typefaces.

Rivers

Look out, also, for *rivers* — the white spaces that run from line to line between words (and sometimes between letters). This could happen with almost any typeface, particularly when broad-bodied type is set justified in narrow columns and when thin-bodied type is set justified in wide columns. (A *justified* text is one in which all the lines of type have been forced into the same length so that they create a box effect. If not justified, the line is said to be *ragged right*.)

6

More on type

Each typeface comes in a *family* of different *weights* (styles). Bookman, for example, comes as Bookman Light, Bookman Medium, and Bookman Demibold, each of which also comes as italic: Bookman Light Italic, Bookman Medium Italic, and Bookman Demibold Italic. Some faces may have extra light or ultra bold weights. You can also find weights that are narrow (*condensed*) or wide (*extended, expanded*).

To avoid monotony, vary the appearance of type on your pages. This can be achieved very effectively if you stay with one family and use, for example, the standard weight for the main text, a bold weight for headings and subheadings, and italics for captions.

Using a second family

If you want a second family, use one that works well with your main text. The trick in creating a balanced page is to find a good contrast rather than a bad match for the typefaces. A "good contrast" is not the same as an "extreme contrast," so be careful in selecting the weight of a face. A light weight Times would be overpowered by a Futura Extra Bold, for example.

You need to study the x-height as well as the various components of key letters to see how two specific faces look together. Palatino and Times Roman are too much alike to be used together, as are Helvetica and Avant Garde. These combinations may give the impression of being mistakes rather than carefully planned partners.

A question of weight

The weight of the face is important. Some light faces look lost on large pages, especially if there are extra-wide margins or other large expanses of white space.

Six families of type

Bookman Light
Bookman Light Italic
Bookman Medium
Bookman Medium Italic
Bookman Demi
Bookman Demi Italic
Bookman Bold
Bookman Bold Italic

Garamond Light
Garamond Light Italic
Garamond Book
Garamond Book Italic
Garamond Bold
Garamond Bold Italic
Garamond Ultra
Garamond Ultra Italic

Helvetica Thin
Helvetica Thin Italic
Helvetica Light
Helvetica Light Italic
Helvetica Medium
Helvetica Medium Italic
Helvetica Bold
Helvetica Bold Italic
Helvetica Black
Helvetica Black Italic
Helvetica Bold Outline

Optima Roman
Optima Roman Italic
Optima Medium
Optima Medium Italic
Optima Bold
Optima Bold Italic
Optima Black
Optima Black Italic

Palatino Roman
Palatino Roman Italic
Palatino Bold
Palatino Bold Italic
PALATINO SMALL CAPS

Times Roman
Times Roman Italic
Times Bold
Times Bold Italic
Times Extra Bold
TIMES SMALL CAPS

A medium face may be more appropriate. Sans serif faces, in particular, appear very light on large spreads since their lack of strokes requires judicious spacing between the letters and words. But beware of creating just the opposite effect by choosing a bold face for solid blocks of text. Its overall effect can be overpowering.

In books of photography (or heavy illustrations) where the text is of less significance, a typeface with a light weight may be better than a heavy one since it is less likely to compete with the photographs for attention.

Pros and cons of sans

Some studies have concluded that sans serif faces are harder to read when set in large blocks of text. Today this is being challenged as more and more publishers print entire books in sans serif, the consensus being that, with careful spacing, these faces are not only easy to read but are also more appropriate for certain books.

Whereas serifs create natural spacing between individual letters, faces without them are dependent on spacing added by the typesetter and, consequently, should be chosen with care. Sans serif faces also need more spacing between the lines. They tend to have a solid, almost rigid appearance and lack the sense of easy rhythm projected by serif faces.

One exception is the elegant Optima, which has a graceful curve in its thick and thin strokes. Two excellent reference books by the award-winning designer Jan V. White — *Editing by design* and *Graphic Design for the Electronic Age* — use Optima throughout as body text.

There is a tendency to think of sans serif faces as contemporary. In fact, the style can be traced back to marble tablets inscribed in ancient Greece in the year 500 BC — hundreds of years before Romans developed letters with serifs. The revival began about 1816, but the faces popular today are of a more recent vintage, Futura appearing in the 1920s, Optima in the 1950s, and Helvetica in the 1960s.

Measuring type with a gauge

An indispensable tool is a *type gauge,* which you can buy at almost any art supply store. There are different brands, the most popular being the Haberule. This is made of a sturdy yellow plastic and is divided into scales from 6-point to 15-point. By placing it on top of

HABERULE "10" TYPE GAUGE

POINT SIZE

AGATE   6   7   8   9   10   11   12

a block of text you can determine the depth of the individual lines or how many lines of a specific type will fit in a given space.

The 12-point scale can also be used to measure picas (12 points = 1 pica) and for this reason it is placed on the outer edge of the gauge.

The Haberule doesn't include 14-, 16-, 18-, or 20-point scales, although you can still get a reading for these by applying the 7, 8, 9 or 10 scales and counting every second unit.

Leading

Text set in a block needs a certain amount of spacing between the lines to keep the characters from flowing into each other. In the old days this was done using strips of lead varying in thickness. Each strip was called a *lead*, and the process was referred to as *leading* (pronounced *ledding*).

The amount of leading was determined by a combination of the x-height of the type and the length of the printed line. A thick face on a long line would need more leading than would a slim face on a short line. And a face with a small x-height that did not reach the full depth of the metal block's face might not need very much leading.

A safe rule of thumb was for the leading to be 20% of the type's point size (e.g., a 2-point lead for a 10-point typeface).

Although the system has changed, and strips of lead are no longer used, the principle still applies and leading lives on. However, the word "leading" is now being replaced by the computerese *inter-line spacing*.

The thickness of leading is measured in points and, because you almost invariably need that space under each line of type, the two measurements are combined. For example, if you have 10-point type on 2-point leading, you say the type is *10 on 12*, expressed as 10/12 (10 point type + 2 point leading = 12 points).

In this example the lines of type align only with the 12-point scale on the Haberule. This tells you that the *baseline to baseline* (i.e., the type's point size when combined with the leading) is 12 points.

A face with a small x-height may not need leading, in which case you would say it is 10/10, or *solid*. Thanks to computers, this gap can be made even narrower, and you can have 10/9½ — called *minus leading*, or *minus linespacing*.

Alice opened the door and found that it led into a small passage, not much larger than a rat-hole: she knelt down and looked along the passage into the loveliest garden you ever saw. How she longed to get out of that dark hall, and wander about among those beds of bright flowers and those cool fountains, but she could not even get her head through the doorway; "and even if my head would go through," thought poor Alice, "it would be of very little use without my shoulders."

An example of too little leading. The typeface — Bookman — has a large x-height, so choice of leading is particularly critical.

Alice opened the door and found that it led into a

small passage, not much larger than a rat-hole:

she knelt down and looked along the passage

into the loveliest garden you ever saw. How she

longed to get out of that dark hall, and wander

about among those beds of bright flowers and

those cool fountains, but she could not even get

her head through the doorway; "and even if my

head would go through," thought poor Alice, "it

would be of very little use without my shoulders."

Here there is too much leading, which causes the eye to jump around the page.

Alice opened the door and found that it led into a small passage, not much larger than a rat-hole: she knelt down and looked along the passage into the loveliest garden you ever saw. How she longed to get out of that dark hall, and wander about among those beds of bright flowers and those cool fountains, but she could not even get her head through the doorway; "and even if my head would go through," thought poor Alice, "it would be of very little use without my shoulders."

This is a more acceptable combination of type and leading.

Alice opened the door and found that it led into a small passage, not much larger than a rat-hole: she knelt down and looked along the passage into the loveliest garden you ever saw. How she longed to get out of that dark hall, and wander about among those cool fountains, but she could not even get her head through the doorway; "and even if my head would go through," thought poor Alice, "it would be of very little use without my shoulders."

If the spacing between letters and words is too tight the text is difficult to read.

This method of measurement is being challenged by modern technology, and many typographers simply measure from *baseline to baseline*. (The *baseline* is the invisible line on which the body of type sits.) Instead of calling it "10/12 type," these people call it "12-point type." However, purists shun this system because the two elements (10-point type,   2-point leading) lose their distinction.

As a guide when determining the amount of leading required, keep in mind the following:

- There should be slightly more space between the lines than between the words.
- The leading should be approximately 20% of the type's point size (e.g., 2-point leading for 10-point type).
- The longer the line of type the more crucial are the choices of x-height and leading.

Popular type sizes

The text of most books is set in either 10- or 12-point type, with 1- or 2-point leading. The final choice of combination will depend on the characteristics of the specific typeface as well as on the length of the line.

Generally, the point size of the type should be about half the pica width of the line — a 10-point type on a 20-pica line, a 12-point type on a 24-pica line, etc.

Word spacing/letter spacing

We also need to consider the amount of space between individual characters (*letter spacing*) and the space between individual words (*word spacing*).

If your text is being set ragged right, the letter spacing will usually take care of itself since the typeface was designed for it to do so. However, if the text is justified, and the characters do not fit the line exactly, spacing will be needed to stretch the line.

Some typesetting systems can be programmed to add spacing between words without adjusting the spacing between the letters. But a large block of text set like this will look awkward: Invariably, you will have rivers running down the page, and your words will be like islands surrounded by too much white space. Or you can add spacing between letters as well as between words. The final effect of this will depend on the typeface. If the typeface is narrow, with fine thin lines, excessive spacing can distort the words and make them less legible.

Even when setting type ragged right some computers produce lines of type that appear too tight or too loose, and adjustments may be needed to make the text easier to read.

Bad letter spacing with lowercase type can endanger legibility and readability more than any other factor. After a lifetime of reading, each of us has developed an innate sense of how our words are structured; we know intuitively how ascenders and descenders shape familiar words, and we are able to recognize them as our eyes skim across the page. When unnatural gaps break down the familiar shape our reading ability is impaired.

The opposite applies to words set entirely in uppercase letters, because of the boxed-in effect created when all letters are of the same height. Here extra letter spacing occasionally has to be added in order to help us with our perception of the words.

The question of what is the appropriate word spacing and letter spacing is a very delicate one and, unless you've had experience in such matters, you cannot be expected to make all the decisions yourself. You, as designer, decide a line or word needs more or less space and let your typesetter figure out how much.

Ems, ens, and quads

Spacing between words and letters is measured either in *ems* (and fractions thereof) or in *units*. These vary according to the point size of a typeface.

In the days of metal type the uppercase letter *M* was considered the standard unit of measure for any given typeface since it usually occupied the entire surface of the block on which it sat. Not surprisingly, perhaps, the unit became known as *em*. This was further divided vertically into ½, ⅓, ¼, ⅕ and ⅙, known respectively as *2–to–the–em space, 3–to–the–em space, 4–to–the–em space, 5–to–the–em space,* and *6–to–the–em space*. The ½ measure is also known as an *en*, or *nut*. For each of these a piece of metal would be inserted wherever a space was required and, because it was shorter than the standard .9186" type-high, it would not print.

The metal block for the *M* space was called a *quad*, and

if you wanted larger spaces you would combine them and refer to them as *2 em quad, 3 em quad,* etc.

In a 10-point type the em would measure 10 points x 10 points, and the en would measure 5 points x 10 points. In a 12-point type the em would measure 12 points x 12 points, and the en would measure 6 points x 12 points, and so on.

So you can see that the spacing would always be in proportion to the actual typeface being used.

This form of measure is still used today, and you can safely indent paragraphs 1 em or 2 em (except on really long lines when you may want to allow more space). Also, 1 en is still considered adequate spacing between words for most faces.

However, because computers can vary the shapes and sizes of individual letters within a font, the letter *M* is no longer considered a reliable yardstick for the new faces being created.

Individual letters are designed on grids divided into vertical units. At one time the standard was 18 units per letter, but as technology advanced more units were required, and now we find some font manufacturers breaking a single letter space into thousands of units.

I don't want to dwell on desktop publishing techniques but I mention this latest method of measurement so the average reader will not feel completely computer illiterate if a typesetter starts speaking this language.

Small capitals

True *small capitals* (or, *small caps*) are not the same as reduced capital letters. They are uppercase letters designed specifically to be the same size as, or slightly larger than, the x-height of lowercase letters.

Not all fonts have small caps, and often typesetters will shrink capital letters to create them. However, with some fonts this can be disastrous because the letters become squished in the process and look ungainly. They will lack the cleanliness and crispness of a true small capital.

If you intend to use small caps in your book you should remember this when selecting a typeface.

Acronyms or initials (e.g., NATO, U.S.) look better on a page when printed in small caps. They do not stand out so awkwardly in a text that consists mainly of lower-case letters.

In the above paragraph I used small capitals. In repeating the paragraph below I used the typeface's normal uppercase letters. See the difference?

Acronyms or initials (e.g., NATO, U.S.) look better on a page when printed in small caps. They do not stand out so awkwardly in a text that consists mainly of lower-case letters.

Also, the ampersand (&) of some fonts looks awkward and you would be better off using the small cap version (&), particularly when it appears between two lower-case words. (In any event, you should generally restrict the use of an ampersand to titles and company names and avoid using it as a substitute for the word "and.")

In this book I use small caps for acronyms and also for emphasis when otherwise I might use capital letters. There are a few exceptions for initials, however, such as state abbreviations accompanying capitalized words in addresses (New York, N.Y., etc.); I retain the normal capitals, because the sudden change to small caps would be inappropriate.

You can combine small caps with normal capitals if you need emphasis for proper nouns or to capitalize the first word of a sentence, or you can use small caps only, as in the adjoining illustrations.

Design & production

Design & production

THE KING AND QUEEN OF HEARTS
Caps and small caps

THE KING AND QUEEN OF HEARTS
All small caps

Aligning and non-aligning numerals

When the time comes to set arabic numerals in type you may find you have a choice of two styles — *Old Style* (also called *non-aligning*) and *Modern* (*aligning*). Some typefaces offer both as alternatives, while others come with one or the other.

Old Style numerals have ascenders and descenders which enable them to blend well with lowercase letters. They also have more personality than rigid Modern numerals, yet they can disturb the balance of a text when set among capital letters.

Modern numerals are designed to be the same height as the capital letters of a typeface and consequently they fit comfortably in a line that is set uppercase. If

ff fi fl ffi ffl The standard f-ligatures set in Utopia Expert.

ff fi fl ffi ffl The same letters set in Palatino.

ff fi fl ffi ffl The same letters set in New Century Schoolbook.
Notice how the top of the f crashes into the dot of the i.

1 2 3 4 5 6 A B C D E F 7 8 9 G H K

Aligning numerals are designed to be the same height as uppercase letters.

1 2 3 4 5 6 a b c d e f 7 8 9 g h k

The ascenders and descenders of non-aligning numerals work well with lowercase letters . . .

1 2 3 4 5 6 A B C D E F 7 8 9 G H K

. . . but not so well with uppercase letters.

1	i	I	11	xi	XI	25	xxv	XXV
2	ii	II	12	xii	XII	30	xxx	XXX
3	iii	III	13	xiii	XIII	35	xxxv	XXXV
4	iv	IV	14	xiv	XIV	40	xl	XL
5	v	V	15	xv	XV	45	xlv	XLV
6	vi	VI	16	xvi	XVI	50	l	L
7	vii	VII	17	xvii	XVII	70	lxx	LXX
8	viii	VIII	18	xviii	XVIII	80	lxxx	LXXX
9	ix	IX	19	xix	XIX	90	xc	XC
10	x	X	20	xx	XX	100	c	C

Roman numerals. Usually the lowercase numerals are used as folios on front matter pages, while uppercase numerals are used to identify parts or sections in manuals.

you have any tabular matter in your book you should use these rather than the Old Style numerals because they are more clearly defined when printed small.

Roman numerals

You can create roman numerals from either lowercase or uppercase letters. Usually lowercase letters are used as folios on front matter pages, while uppercase ones are used to identify parts of technical manuals.

The basic principle is that a lower numeral (and you do need to think of each letter as a numeral) following a greater one will add to the value of the greater numeral; a lower numeral appearing in front of a greater one will be deducted. If you remember this — and a few key numerals — you should be able to figure out the rest.

Fractions

I have noticed a trend among desktop publishers to replace fractions with decimals even when decimals are not called for. I assume this is because, with many of the programs, it is easier to type 1.5 and 2.75 than to enter 1½ and 2¾. These fractions usually do require additional keystrokes and extra time which, for some people, is sufficient reason to opt for decimals.

There are occasions when decimals must be used, as in most scientific and medical material. Nevertheless, the friendly little fractions still have their uses, and it is sad to see them replaced by decimals merely because they require a few extra strokes on a computer keyboard.

If you want fractions you should be able to get them. Just let your typesetter know of your preference. If you are setting your own type, take the few extra moments to create them. Your book will look better for it.

Ligatures and diphthongs

When I first saw *f-ligatures* (ff, fi, fl, ffi, ffl) on sheets of press-on type I assumed they belonged only in non-English words, probably because they were usually accompanied by characters such as ü, é, â, å, ç, ñ, ø, and š. Enlarged, they always looked alien and some-what forbidding.

Yet when I began studying typography I realized that ligatures had been used in many of the books I had been reading all my life, but I hadn't been aware of them. Ironically, they may have helped make those texts easier to read.

Diphthongs (Æ, æ, Œ, œ) are also considered ligatures but are rarely seen now. Whereas the f-ligatures were created to conserve space, diphthongs represent actual sounds or pronunciations in certain words. But many words that at one time were printed with diphthongs have changed their spelling. When did you last see the word "encyclopedia" written as "encyclopædia," or "ecology" as "œcology"?

Diphthongs are included with most computer typefaces, and if you need them in your book you should check with your typesetter. Desktop publishers should look closely at the options when buying new faces.

The major desktop publishing programs and laser printers can print f-ligatures without too much effort on the typesetter's part. However, only a few computer typefaces have them at present. I suspect more will be available as the demand grows.

It is up to you, as publisher and designer, to determine whether or not the style will be used. It may help if you look closely at how your typeface prints lowercase words containing fi or ffi combinations. Does the f have a little dot that looks awkward beside the dot of the i?

Did you notice that the text of this book has ligatures?

Color of type

All of the things discussed in this chapter can affect the way your printed page will look. In combination, they create what typographers call *color of type*.

A trained eye will see the combination of all these elements as tones of gray. The more evenly balanced they are, the more harmonious the page; and the more harmonious the page, the easier it is to read.

Try looking at a page through squinted eyes, or while holding it upside down: You will be less tempted to read what is written and can concentrate on the overall grayness as the various weights of type blend with the patches of white on the page.

7

Choosing a typeface

In selecting a typeface you need only two criteria:

- Is it appropriate for your book?
- Is it legible and readable?

Is it appropriate?

To be appropriate, the typeface should reflect the mood of your book. It should also look comfortable on the page, which in itself should suit the character of your manuscript. Every element — especially the type-face — should work in harmony with what the book is all about. Remember DICODOB (Does It Complement Overall Design Of Book?).

When you are looking at typefaces try to imagine them being used in your book. Right away you will see that many of them can be rejected without much thought. They just do not feel right for the mood you want. You may end up with three or four to choose from, and you probably could select any one of those.

It may be easier to decide which typefaces are NOT appropriate rather than which ones are. If your book is a historical novel you would not select a twentieth century sans serif face, for example. Similarly, you would not select a heavy, ponderous typeface for a book of humor, or for a book intended as light reading.

Consider the age of your audience, and do not use a slim-bodied type if your book is aimed at senior citizens or very young readers.

When I said the type should look comfortable on the page I was reiterating what I had said earlier: Light faces look skimpy on large pages with wide borders, and heavy faces look crowded on small pages crammed with text. As a rule, use faces with larger set-widths for large pages (e.g., 8½" x 11") and the taller and slimmer x-heights for small vertical pages (e.g., 6" x 9").

Is it legible and readable?

Legibility and readability form the second criterion for selecting a typeface. These two words may seem the same but they are not.

- *Legibility* concerns the ease and ability with which the letters of text can be recognized.
- *Readability* concerns the ease and ability with which the text can be read.

Factors involved include the size of type in relation to space around it, the length of a line of text in relation to space between it and the lines above and below it, the shape of the individual characters, and the texture and color of the paper on which the type is printed.

A 6-point type could be readable and legible if used as a short caption, or a brief footnote, or even as a small block of text on the copyright page. But if that same 6-point type extended across the full width of your text area, and continued for an entire page, it could not be read easily because the individual characters would no longer be readable at a normal reading pace. The eye can take such small type only in limited doses. Nevertheless, the individual words are still *legible* — you can recognize what each character is, even though it may take you all day to get to the end of one page.

When some faces are reduced or enlarged they become distorted — the letter forms lose their crispness and become less legible. This is one of the reasons why you should not make your final decision until you have seen a typeface set at the size you intend to use it, with its correct spacing and leading.

To justify or not to justify?

That is the question! Although we are accustomed to reading books with lines of equal length, few people other than designers and fine printers are aware that a poorly justified text can slow down a reader's pace. By "poorly justified" I mean those lines of type that have been either packed too tight or stretched out with too much spacing, in order to justify them. Bad choice of typefaces is another cause.

A page that has been justified correctly, with the love and care a fine printer is capable of giving it, can be a joy to look at and to read. The spacing has been apportioned according to the basic rules of legibility and readability, rather than to fill the line. There is an easy rhythm flowing through the entire page, allowing the reader to absorb the meaning of the words rather than be distracted by the words themselves.

Hyphenation, or unsightly gaps. One consideration to bear in mind when deciding whether or not to justify is the visual effect created by hyphenated words. If you do not justify your lines then it is no longer necessary to break so many words, thus avoiding an ugly cluster of hyphenations on the right edge of the text.

But do not fall into the trap of believing that no words need be hyphenated if you do not justify the text. This tactic could result, instead, in a cluster of wide gaps, which look almost as bad as too many hyphens. You are better off compromising and allowing selective hyphenation. When not justifying your text you should decide on a minimum line length — one that will be, say, not more than 2 or 3 picas shorter than the edge of the text area.

Also, watch out for more than two or three consecutive lines of exactly the same length. The principle should be "all or none," and if you choose not to justify your lines then you have to make sure they do not justify themselves by default.

Indenting paragraphs. By now you have noticed that my text is not justified. But have you noticed that I do not indent the first line of each paragraph? I do this so as to have at least one straight, uninterrupted edge to the block of text. Even my headings, subheadings, and bullet items are aligned on the left to accentuate that clean line. Instead of indenting I separate each paragraph with an extra line space. This is not to say you must not indent paragraphs if you do not justify your text. It is merely an example of the options you have.

Deleting the indents may be acceptable when the text is ragged right, but when it is justified and you have page after page of solid blocks of type it would not be a good choice. You need an occasional variant to prevent the text from becoming ponderous. This variant can be provided by indenting your paragraphs 1 em or 2 em. When you do this you can have the same amount of leading between paragraphs as between lines.

It is customary when indenting paragraphs not to indent the first paragraph of a chapter, nor the first paragraph after a subheading, even when all other paragraphs are indented.

It is also customary EITHER to indent your paragraphs OR to leave extra line spacing between paragraphs, but not both.

The theme of your book may also be a major consideration in deciding whether to justify your text. That earlier book of mine about two dogs was intended to convey a sense of mid-nineteenth century — a feeling that would have been destroyed if the text had been set ragged right. The book you are now studying, however, is a manual for the late twentieth century, with references to computers and technology not available at any earlier period. Hence I felt justified in not justifying.

The question, then, is one of design, since it will affect the overall appearance of your page as well as the mood of your book.

Hanging punctuation

To a fine printer, a block of text is not truly justified if there are gaps at the ends of lines where certain punctuation marks appear. For example, a comma, an em dash, or even a period at the end of a line will create a tiny break in an otherwise straight right-hand edge. To avoid this, that fine printer will *hang* the offending mark outside the text area and, if necessary, replace a dash with a smaller mark so that it is not so obvious.

This is referred to as *hung punctuation*, and it is not new to typography. Johann Gutenberg used it when he hand-set the type for his Bible in the fifteenth century.

When Hermann Zapf, the renowned type designer and calligrapher, adjudicated the Association of American University Presses' 1986 Book Show, he wrote in the catalog about one of the finalists:

> One improvement in the typesetting would have been to use hung punctuation to make it perfect. Is this so difficult to do in the United States? In order to have top-quality typesetting, hung punctuation should be standard, and it could be implemented through aesthetic programs so there would not be a significant overall increase in composition costs.

You may not feel it necessary to go to this extreme with

your first book, especially since it could add to the cost of typesetting. But at least you now know about it, and one day you may incorporate it as part of your house typesetting style.

Selecting the typeface for you

By now you should be in a better position to decide what typeface you want for your book. To help you, I include at the end of this chapter eight faces that are suitable for books. Study them carefully, keeping in mind issues I have raised. But do not limit yourself to these eight. There are others.

If you are setting the type yourself I'm sure that you are aware of the great variety of faces available for your system. Computer magazines provide a constant flow of information about current and upcoming faces. Also, you can write to type manufacturers such as Adobe Systems or Bitstream and request copies of their catalogs.

But if you want a typesetter to do the work for you, look for someone who can help you with your choice. Most professional typesetters prepare a *type style book* showing the different faces they can set for you. Some of these books will consist solely of the different fonts; more elaborate ones will include the fonts plus examples of how each will look when set as a block of text. If you want a face that is not included in the style book, the typesetter may buy it for you once you secure your order.

Some typesetters will sell these books to you, some will give them to you, others will let you look at them only in the shop. In any case, they are intended for you, a potential customer, to study.

Before making your final decision, ask the typesetter to set a block of text in each of the faces you are considering, with the leading you have in mind. For an accurate picture, you will need to have the block set in exactly the same line length you will use in your book. If you have a lot of extracts you will need samples showing how they will look in their smaller size indented within your text.

If cost is a factor at this stage, it may be cheaper to have the typesetter set a block using some text already in the computer instead of typing new text. This way you may be able to get enough type to fill the two-page spread of your master layout, and thus get an even better idea of how the type will look on the page. After all, you only want to test it for its legibility and readability, which can be determined whether the words are yours or someone else's.

Caveat emptor

Do not select a typeface from the style book of one typesetter and expect to get the same results from another typesetter.

Now that type is generated by many different methods nobody can guarantee that, for example, Palatino produced by one typesetter will look exactly like Palatino produced by another. The degree of crispness can vary with the amount of exposure given by different photo-typesetters, and different printing machines will create subtle variations in the structure of the characters.

Consequently, you should know exactly how your typesetter's system will produce the face you want before making up your mind.

This is something to remember when, at a later date, you are going into a new printing and need to make corrections and additions to the text. Be sure you use the same typesetter or, if not, that you find a good match for the type already set on your pages. Type-setters periodically upgrade their equipment, so you should check even if you go back to the same person.

Remember the criteria

When you get the sample blocks of type, hold them in position under your layout guide to see how they look. Although photocopies will have their uses later, at this stage you have to work with the originals if you want to gauge the true personality of your design. Look carefully at one, then another, and make up your mind. Throughout, ask yourself:

- Is it appropriate?
- Is it legible and readable?

A few sample typefaces

On the following pages are samples of eight typefaces suitable for books. All text blocks are set 10½/12.

Baskerville

Roman

The March Hare took the watch and looked at it gloomily: then he dipped it into his cup of tea, and looked at it again: but he could think of nothing better to say than his first remark, "It was the best butter, you know."

Italic

The March Hare took the watch and looked at it gloomily: then he dipped it into his cup of tea, and looked at it again: but he could think of nothing better to say than his first remark, "It was the best butter, you know."

Bold

The March Hare took the watch and looked at it gloomily: then he dipped it into his cup of tea, and looked at it again: but he could think of nothing better to say than his first remark, "It was the best butter, you know."

Bold Italic

The March Hare took the watch and looked at it gloomily: then he dipped it into his cup of tea, and looked at it again: but he could think of nothing better to say than his first remark, "It was the best butter, you know."

A B C D E F G H I J K L M N O P Q R S T U V W X Y Z

a b c d e f g h i j k l m n o p q r s t u v w x y z

1 2 3 4 5 6 7 8 9 0 á à â ä ã a̧ £ ß $ ¢ # % & ? ¡ ! ¿ * ( ) [ ] " , " : ;

Bookman

Light

The March Hare took the watch and looked at it
gloomily: then he dipped it into his cup of tea, and
looked at it again: but he could think of nothing better
to say than his first remark, "It was the best butter,
you know."

Italic

*The March Hare took the watch and looked at it gloomi-
ly: then he dipped it into his cup of tea, and looked at it
again: but he could think of nothing better to say than
his first remark, "It was the best butter, you know."*

Demibold

**The March Hare took the watch and looked at it
gloomily: then he dipped it into his cup of tea, and
looked at it again: but he could think of nothing
better to say than his first remark, "It was the best
butter, you know."**

Demibold Italic

***The March Hare took the watch and looked at it
gloomily: then he dipped it into his cup of tea,
and looked at it again: but he could think of nothing better to say than his first remark, "It was the
best butter, you know."***

A B C D E F G H I J K L M N O P Q R S T U V W X Y Z

a b c d e f g h i j k l m n o p q r s t u v w x y z

1 2 3 4 5 6 7 8 9 0 ~ ! @ # $ % & * ( ) [ ] " , " ? : ;

Garamond

Roman

The March Hare took the watch and looked at it gloomily: then he dipped it into his cup of tea, and looked at it again: but he could think of nothing better to say than his first remark, ''It was the best butter, you know.''

Italic

The March Hare took the watch and looked at it gloomily: then he dipped it into his cup of tea, and looked at it again: but he could think of nothing better to say than his first remark, ''It was the best butter, you know.''

Bold

The March Hare took the watch and looked at it gloomily: then he dipped it into his cup of tea, and looked at it again: but he could think of nothing better to say than his first remark, ''It was the best butter, you know.''

Bold Italic

The March Hare took the watch and looked at it gloomily: then he dipped it into his cup of tea, and looked at it again: but he could think of nothing better to say than his first remark, ''It was the best butter, you know.''

ABCDEFGHIJKLMNOPQRSTUVWXYZ

abcdefghijklmnopqrstuvwxyz

1234567890!#✔$%&*()[] − ± ÷ × = †‡§@'',''?!:;

Helvetica

Helvetica

The March Hare took the watch and looked at it gloomily:
then he dipped it into his cup of tea, and looked at it again:
but he could think of nothing better to say than his first
remark, "It was the best butter, you know."

Oblique

The March Hare took the watch and looked at it gloomily:
then he dipped it into his cup of tea, and looked at it again:
but he could think of nothing better to say than his first
remark, "It was the best butter, you know."

Bold

The March Hare took the watch and looked at it gloomi-
ly: then he dipped it into his cup of tea, and looked at it
again: but he could think of nothing better to say than
his first remark, "It was the best butter, you know."

Bold Oblique

The March Hare took the watch and looked at it gloomi-
ly: then he dipped it into his cup of tea, and looked at it
again: but he could think of nothing better to say than
his first remark, "It was the best butter, you know."

ABCDEFGHIJKLMNOPQRSTUVWXYZ

abcdefghijklmnopqrstuvwxyz

1234567890 ~ ! @ # $ % & * ( ) [ ] " , " ? : ;

Optima

Roman

The March Hare took the watch and looked at it gloomily:
then he dipped it into his cup of tea, and looked at it again:
but he could think of nothing better to say than his first
remark, "It was the best butter, you know."

Italic

*The March Hare took the watch and looked at it gloomily:
then he dipped it into his cup of tea, and looked at it again:
but he could think of nothing better to say than his first remark,
"It was the best butter, you know."*

Bold

**The March Hare took the watch and looked at it gloomily:
then he dipped it into his cup of tea, and looked at it again:
but he could think of nothing better to say than his first
remark, "It was the best butter, you know."**

Bold Italic

***The March Hare took the watch and looked at it gloomily:
then he dipped it into his cup of tea, and looked at it again:
but he could think of nothing better to say than his first
remark, "It was the best butter, you know."***

ABCDEFGHIJKLMNOPQRSTUVWXYZ

abcdefghijklmnopqrstuvwxyz

1234567890!# ✓ $ % & * ()[] − ± ÷ × = † ‡ § @ " , " ?!:;

Palatino

Roman

The March Hare took the watch and looked at it gloomily:
then he dipped it into his cup of tea, and looked at it again:
but he could think of nothing better to say than his first
remark, "It was the best butter, you know."

Italic

*The March Hare took the watch and looked at it gloomily: then
he dipped it into his cup of tea, and looked at it again: but he
could think of nothing better to say than his first remark, "It was
the best butter, you know."*

Bold

**The March Hare took the watch and looked at it gloomi-
ly: then he dipped it into his cup of tea, and looked at it
again: but he could think of nothing better to say than
his first remark, "It was the best butter, you know."**

Bold Italic

***The March Hare took the watch and looked at it gloomily:
then he dipped it into his cup of tea, and looked at it
again: but he could think of nothing better to say than his
first remark, "It was the best butter, you know."***

A B C D E F G H I J K L M N O P Q R S T U V W X Y Z

a b c d e f g h i j k l m n o p q r s t u v w x y z

1 2 3 4 5 6 7 8 9 0 ~ ! @ # $ % & * ( ) [ ] " , " ' ? : ;

Times

Times

The March Hare took the watch and looked at it gloomily: then he dipped it into his cup of tea, and looked at it again: but he could think of nothing better to say than his first remark, "It was the best butter, you know."

Italic

The March Hare took the watch and looked at it gloomily: then he dipped it into his cup of tea, and looked at it again: but he could think of nothing better to say than his first remark, "It was the best butter, you know."

Bold

The March Hare took the watch and looked at it gloomily: then he dipped it into his cup of tea, and looked at it again: but he could think of nothing better to say than his first remark, "It was the best butter, you know."

Bold Italic

The March Hare took the watch and looked at it gloomily: then he dipped it into his cup of tea, and looked at it again: but he could think of nothing better to say than his first remark, "It was the best butter, you know."

A B C D E F G H I J K L M N O P Q R S T U V W X Y Z

a b c d e f g h i j k l m n o p q r s t u v w x y z

1 2 3 4 5 6 7 8 9 0 ~ ! @ # $ % & * ( ) [ ] " , " ? : ;

Utopia

Regular

The March Hare took the watch and looked at it gloomily: then he dipped it into his cup of tea, and looked at it again: but he could think of nothing better to say than his first remark, "It was the best butter, you know."

Italic

The March Hare took the watch and looked at it gloomily: then he dipped it into his cup of tea, and looked at it again: but he could think of nothing better to say than his first remark, "It was the best butter, you know."

Bold

The March Hare took the watch and looked at it gloomily: then he dipped it into his cup of tea, and looked at it again: but he could think of nothing better to say than his first remark, "It was the best butter, you know."

Bold italic

The March Hare took the watch and looked at it gloomily: then he dipped it into his cup of tea, and looked at it again: but he could think of nothing better to say than his first remark, "It was the best butter, you know."

A B C D E F G H I J K L M N O P Q R S T U V W X Y Z

a b c d e f g h i j k l m n o p q r s t u v w x y z

1 2 3 4 5 6 7 8 9 0 @ # $ £ § ‡ % & * ( ) [ ] ? " , " : ;

8

Display type

Large typefaces used for titles, headings, subheadings, etc., are known collectively as *display type*. Normally they are modifications of text faces, although there are also a number of ornamental faces that are created specifically for this use. As the word implies, they are for display: They are the signposts that lead us to specific sections of the text, letting us know what we can expect to find there.

Generally, display type sizes are 18-point or larger. Type smaller than 18-point is considered text type.

If we want to stress the importance of a statement while using a typewriter we automatically hit the shift key and type the whole thing in capital letters. But to continue using the uppercase in this way now that we have access to a multitude of faces and their built-in range of styles (bold, italic, light, condensed, etc.) is not only shamefully restricting but also draws attention to our ignorance. That ignorance becomes even more apparent if we fail to make certain adjustments to letter spacing and word spacing in our headings.

If you are working with a competent professional type-setter you will not need to make all these decisions yourself. Nevertheless, it is in your interest to know these things so that when you check the galleys you can watch out for them. It is impossible to set any hard and fast rules because of the great variety of typefaces available, and in the end it comes down to a gut feeling.

Basically, you need to ensure that spacing APPEARS to be consistent. I stress "appears" because again we are in a situation in which images play tricks on our eyes. This applies in particular to uppercase letters since they often lack the natural spacing that most lowercase letters have.

SLATE
SLATE

Before and after kerning.

Yo
We
To
Tr
Ta
Wo
Tu
Tw
Ya
Te
P.
Ty
Wa
yo
we
T.
Y.
TA
PA
WA

The Top 20 kerns, according to
Frank J. Roman's *TypEncyclopedia*.

Kerning

Certain combinations of letters require *kerning* — that is, the gap between them has to be reduced to prevent their appearing to be farther apart than they are.

Pay particular attention when adjacent words bring together two vertical strokes (e.g., ND): You will need to add a sliver of space. Look also at words in which two open letters sit side by side and create an unusually wide gap (e.g., TA): You will need to reduce the space slightly.

In the days of metal type the typesetter would usually kern only when the crucial combinations appeared in the larger type sizes used for headings. He — and in those days it was almost certainly "he" — would cut indentations into the two blocks of type, thus enabling them to fit together like the pieces of a jigsaw puzzle. Today, computers are programmed to kern even the smallest type used in bodies of text, and typesetters are creating combinations that were not necessary before.

In *The TypEncyclopedia*, Frank J. Romano takes issue with this practice. He points out that most computer systems can kern more than 200 character pairs automatically and he asks where one stops without creating inconsistencies. There are twenty primary pairs, he says, and "if you cannot kern infinitely, then you might as well stay with the top 20 — anything after that is a numbers game."

Watch word spacing

If you adjust the space between letters, be sure also to check what happens to the space between words. Obviously you need more space between words than between letters, and even more space between lines (*leading*).

Usually you do not need to adjust the spacing of lowercase letters. And you may not need to change letter spacing if you are using a condensed type.

Uppercase and lowercase

You need not use all capitals to emphasize a point in your headings. Emphasis can be achieved effectively by choosing a typeface that is bolder or more decorative. It can also be achieved by the way you position the words on the page.

Nor do you need to capitalize every word in a heading. Award-winning designer Jan V. White is particularly adamant about this point and in his book *Editing by design* he writes:

> Never Set Headlines Using Capital Initials And Lowercase On Every Word — unless your intention is to create visual hiccups.

A word that normally requires a capital initial (a proper noun, for example) should, of course, retain it. Sometimes you will want to capitalize one or two specific words for emphasis and that too is permissible. Otherwise, begin each word of a heading with a lowercase letter as you would in normal text, and capitalize only the first word. Usually the heading is meant to be read as a statement, so why not set it like one?

Placement of headings

Chapter titles and other headings take on different connotations according to their position on the page. Traditionally they are centered from left to right, giving a symmetrical appearance to the page. The effect is one of dignity and orderliness — except to people who think of it as dull and boring.

When centering anything on a page, use as a guide the center point of the overall image area, not the center of the page itself.

Place the heading flush left so that it aligns with the left edge of your text area and it takes on a more commanding position — especially if the lines are short and you have a generous amount of space on the right.

Place it flush right, and let it fall ragged left, and it has a totally different feeling. However, you should consider this only if your text is justified, or else the total effect will become jagged.

More than one line

If the heading is longer than one line — or if it looks too skimpy as one line — be careful how you break it. Do not break merely to create a good visual effect. Remember, these are words that have to be read and understood instantly. By thoughtlessly separating two key words you can distort their meaning, or misplace an important emphasis. Sometimes it is necessary to put on your editor's cap and change a word or two.

With a two-line heading the second line should be shorter than the first. This not only makes it easier for your reader to get back to the beginning of the text, but it helps to create a neater effect for the whole page.

Rules, from hairline to 72 points

Straight lines are called *rules* and are measured in points or fractions of points. If you want to be less specific you can refer to them as either *fine, medium,* or *thick.* They come in a variety of thicknesses, from very fine (*hairline* is only ¼ point thick) to a solid ribbon of black measuring 72 points.

Use them as a design element, or to emphasize specific portions of text, or to separate columns of numbers. Run them horizontally, vertically, or diagonally. You can also make boxes out of them to put around blocks of text or around illustrations.

But do not overuse them. Too many can be distracting; if too thick, they can be overpowering. Use the fine lines sparingly, if at all. They tend to break down or disappear altogether when printed on some laser printers.

One of the few rules of *rules* is that they should complement the text that accompanies them. They should not overpower or be overpowered by the text. Use the thickness of upright strokes in the typeface as a benchmark.

9

Folios to footnotes

Book design is more than selecting type and laying out
pages. It reaches into the blocks of text and affects the
way paragraphs begin and lines end. It determines the
relationship between headings and subheadings. Not
even the page number escapes careful scrutiny, as you
will see in this chapter.

Extracts

An *extract* is a lengthy passage from another source,
too long to be put in quotation marks within a paragraph of the text but still requiring clear identification
as a quotation.

One way is to indent the entire extract slightly from the
left margin and set it in a smaller type than the body of
the text. Another way is to center it within the text area
(i.e., indented left and right) and set it in smaller type.
In either case, you should reduce the leading between
the lines (because the type is smaller) while slightly
increasing the leading above and below the extract so
that it is quite clearly separated from the text.

It is not a good idea to use italics for an extract, particularly if it is several lines long, because that would
slow your reader's pace. For the same reason, you
should not choose a size of type much smaller than
your regular text. A difference of one or two points will
be sufficient.

You can start a lengthy quotation within the body of
text and continue it as an extract. In this case you place
quotation marks around the first section, then add a
few words of text before beginning the extract format.

An extract is not enclosed within quotation marks. If a
quotation appears within the extract it is treated as any

John Muir felt that people should spend more time climbing mountains than reading about them. "No amount of word-making will ever make a single soul to *know* these mountains," he wrote in 1872.

> One day's exposure to mountains is better than cartloads of books. See how willingly Nature poses herself upon photographers' plates. No earthy chemicals are so sensitive as those of the human soul. All that is required is exposure, and purity of material.

Today hikers are able to visit Mount Muir, Muir Lake, Muir Grove of Big Trees, Muir Woods, and the Muir Trail.

If you begin a lengthy quotation within the body of text and then print the bulk of it as an extract, use quotation marks only on the first section and not on the extract.

John Muir felt that people should spend more time climbing mountains than reading about them. "No amount of word-making will ever make a single soul to *know* these mountains," he wrote in 1872.

> One day's exposure to mountains is better than cartloads of books. See how willingly Nature poses herself upon photographers' plates. No earthy chemicals are so sensitive as those of the human soul. All that is required is exposure, and purity of material.

Today hikers are able to visit Mount Muir, Muir Lake, Muir Grove of Big Trees, Muir Woods, and the Muir Trail.

An extract can be indented both left and right, as in the first example, or only from the left, as in this example.

John Muir felt that people should spend more time climbing mountains than reading about them. "No amount of word-making will ever make a single soul to *know* these mountains," he wrote in 1872.

> *One day's exposure to mountains is better than cartloads of books. See how willingly Nature poses herself upon photographers' plates. No earthy chemicals are so sensitive as those of the human soul. All that is required is exposure, and purity of material.*

Today hikers are able to visit Mount Muir, Muir Lake, Muir Grove of Big Trees, Muir Woods, and the Muir Trail.

Using italics rather than a smaller size of the body typeface tends to slow your reader's pace.

other, and is enclosed in double quotation marks. A quotation within that quotation will, as usual, require single quotation marks.

If the extract is a lengthy quotation from a poem it should be centered, and aligned in the same way as the original. However, you could also run all lines together, using slashes to indicate the line breaks. Usually the names of the poem and the poet are printed slightly off center beneath the extract, using italics.

If your book has only a few extracts, you could include their sources within the text itself, or italicize them in parentheses immediately following the extract. Or you can use footnotes, with either superscript figures, asterisks, daggers, or double daggers.

If you have many extracts, the best way to identify each one is with a superscript figure referring your reader to notes in the back of the book.

Footnotes

There are two kinds of footnotes: those that explain something within the text, and those that refer the reader to the source of a quoted item.

The first should be avoided whenever possible, preferably by including the explanation in the body of text. However, there may be occasions when an explanation is of such a technical or scholarly nature that to include it in the text would create too much of a distraction; the reader may prefer a more propitious moment to read it.

If the reference footnote is not much longer than a few words it could be placed at the foot of the page in small type — usually 2 points smaller than body text.

Whether you choose a superscript figure or an asterisk to link the footnote with its reference point in the text will depend on how many footnotes you have. If there are several on a page, use superscript figures; if there is only one, use an asterisk.

If a footnote is longer than a few words, possibly including a comment about the source, you would be better off placing it at the back with notes.

However, some people disapprove of the mixing of explanatory notes with reference notes. You may want to bear this in mind when organizing your footnotes.

Whenever possible, the last line of a footnote appearing on a text page should align with the last line of type on the opposite page.

If it is a very long footnote you can run it over onto the next page. In doing so, use a fine rule to separate the continued portion of the footnote from the main text.

➤   *See pages 15:125–26 concerning notes in the back matter.*

Page numbers

A page number is a *folio.* If it appears at the bottom of a page it is a *drop folio.* If no number appears, that is a *blind folio.*

- 1, 2, 3, 4, 5, etc. are *arabic* numerals.
- i, ii, iii, iv, v, etc. are *roman* numerals.

With some typefaces you have a choice of Old Style numerals (called *non-aligning*) or Modern numerals (*aligning*).

➤   *See Chapter 6 for more information about numerals.*

The importance of folios will vary with different types of books. Novels, for example, have less need for them than a reference book. In Chapter 3 I indicated where they should be placed on the page. Here I try to answer other questions:

- On what page do you start the numbering?
- Do you use arabic or roman numerals?
- When, and why, do you not include a page number?
- What point size should the numbers be?

On what page do you start numbering? The very first page (the flyleaf) is considered number one. Because this is a right-hand page all odd numbers in the book will appear on right-hand pages, and all even numbers on left-hand pages. Do not be confused by the endpaper of a hardcover book. That thicker sheet of paper has been added to support the heavy cover board, to hold it onto the book itself, and is not assigned a page number.

Arabic or roman? In the days when every letter for every word was set by hand, the typesetter needed to start work on a book as early as possible. This often meant not waiting for the introduction or preface to be written, since usually these were not complete until after the book itself was finished. The problem was solved by using a different set of numerals (lowercase roman letters) for the front matter.

Today, thanks to computer technology, we can make alterations in the text and can change page numbers up to a few hours before production. Yet some publishers cling to tradition and use roman numerals in the front matter. The choice is yours.

There really is no great advantage to using the roman numerals other than for their aesthetic value. However, they do have one disadvantage: Some people assume that the total number of pages in a book is indicated by the final folio, forgetting the pages with roman numerals in the front matter and the unnumbered blank pages at the back.

If you use both roman and arabic, counting for the arabic numerals starts with the first page of the main text. This could be the first section title or part-title page or, if you do not have these, then the first page of the body text. Remember that the first number must be on a right-hand page.

➤ *See page 6:48 for arabic equivalents of roman numerals.*

When not to number a page. Regardless of whether you are using roman or arabic numerals, no folio should appear until after the copyright page. From that point on, publishers make up their own minds where to start. Purists hold out until the second page of the foreword or preface, whichever comes first. Others start as early as the copyright page. Whichever page you start with should be numbered as if all preceding pages had been numbered.

One reason not to number the earlier pages is that they are display pages where every piece of type becomes an element of design. Why put a number there anyway? They are not pages you would turn to for reference.

The question of aesthetics comes into play again with other display pages, such as half-title pages or section title pages, and even blank versos. Most designers do not put folios on any of these. Nor do they put running heads on these pages.

Size of the folio. Generally the folio should be printed 2 points larger than the body text. For a reference book in which your readers may need to locate specific pages in a hurry it is a good idea to use a bold face.

➤ *See page 3:20 concerning placement of folios.*

Identifying signatures

In some older books you will see a single letter printed in the bottom margin on certain pages. This was used as a guide to keep the signatures in their correct order when the book was bound; the letter *c* was printed on the first page of the third signature, *d* on the first page of the fourth, and so on through the book.

The errata slip

Writing in the magazine *Vanity Fair* a few years ago, Jessica Mitford mourned the passing of the *errata slip*, that small piece of paper that brought to your attention, and subsequently corrected, errors in the book. Describing it as "once a hallmark of meticulous publishing," the author of *The American Way of Death* went on to complain, "One never sees an errata insert these days."

The sad part of this, of course, is not that books no longer contain typographical errors but that publishers apparently do not feel any obligation to correct them for the benefit of the reader.

Admittedly, the problem is exacerbated by the speed with which books are produced today; there is less chance an error will be spotted before the books reach the stores, and no time at all to delay distribution while an errata slip is printed and inserted. And we all realize that increasing labor costs have depleted many publishing houses of the once-obligatory staff of proofreaders. But even allowing for the fact that nobody enjoys admitting mistakes, I suspect there is now a certain couldn't-care-less attitude among publishers.

Often the errors are slight, and, particularly in the case of misspelled esoteric words, they may cause no hindrance to a reader. But there are times when the error can cause confusion, challenging the credibility of the book as a whole. These are the occasions when you, as a publisher, should take whatever action is necessary to make amends.

In the first printing of my book *Bummer & Lazarus* the

page numbers listed in the glossary are fourteen pages off. During the pasteup process the pages had been numbered with arabic numerals from the first page, even though I had requested roman numerals for the front matter. That error was spotted, and corrected, but not before I was handed a set of proofs from which I entered the folios into the glossary. I did not notice the mistake until the book was already printed.

Because of the nature of the error, I decided to insert an errata slip. But even that needed to be compatible with the design of the book. I used the same typeface and a similar paper stock. To keep it from falling out in the bookstore I *tipped* it in against the first page of the glossary, using a slim strip of double-sided tape.

The reaction has been interesting. People unaccustomed to seeing such an admission of error are at first confused by it. But bibliophiles recognize it for what it is: "a hallmark of meticulous printing."

If you need one of these slips, use the appropriate Latin word in your heading: The correction of one error is *erratum*; the correction of two or more errors is *errata*.

ERRATA					
All page numbers of glossary are off by 14.					
For	*Read*	*For*	*Read*	*For*	*Read*
16	2	48	34	64	50
39	25	50	36	70	56
40	26	51	37	72	58
47	33	61	47	81	67
		62	48		

Widows and orphans

A *widow* is a very short line appearing at the TOP of a page or column — usually the last words of a paragraph that began on the previous page.

An *orphan* is a very short line appearing at the BOTTOM of a page or column.

These are the most prevalent definitions of the words. You may hear *widow* used to describe ANY incomplete line, as at the end of a paragraph, and you may even hear the two definitions being reversed — orphan at the top of the page, widow at the bottom.

Ideally, the first line of text on a page should be one complete line. When a widow appears the line is broken, upsetting the balance. If possible, ask the author to add a few words in order to fill the line, or to delete a few words so that the offending words can be pulled back to an earlier page or column.

Another solution is to reset the paragraph so that more, or less, word/letter spacing is given. But this also should be done with care to avoid lines looking too *open* (too much space) or too *close* (too little space).

Some publishers insist on having a complete line along the top, and they will not place even the first line of a paragraph there because it is indented. Others are willing to accept lines that are more than three-quarters full. This is one of those areas where you, as publisher, have to establish a house rule. When you do, be sure to let your typesetter and page layout person know what the rule is.

Even when text is not justified, a widow can sometimes upset the appearance of a page.

Word-breaks

A *word-break* is a word that is hyphenated at the end of a line. Assuming the breaks are grammatically correct (if in doubt, check your dictionary), there is nothing wrong UNLESS:

- they appear on several consecutive lines, or
- half the word appears on one page and the other half on the next.

There was a time when publishers would not break a word at the foot of any page, but now some allow a word-break from the bottom of a left-hand page to the top of a right-hand page because it still appears on the same spread. Ideally, you should never expect your reader to turn a page to find the second half of a word.

A cluster of hyphens at the edge of a text area not only spoils the overall appearance of a page but can also aggravate a reader.

Most publishing houses have a rule limiting the number of consecutive lines ending in hyphens to two or three. There are occasions when it is difficult to adhere to this rule, especially if text is justified, because by adjusting one set of word-breaks we often create another cluster farther down the page. Nevertheless, in the end you will be glad you took the extra time.

Decide what your style is, and stick with it.

➤ *See Chapter 7 concerning unjustified text.*

Subheadings

Usually a chapter deals with one specific topic which is identified by the main heading (chapter title) and is then broken into subdivisions, each of which has a *subheading.* Apart from their importance as signposts defining the topic, subheadings play an integral part in the overall design of a book since they help break up an otherwise solid mass of text on each page.

Subheadings are generally set flush against the left edge of the text area and are printed 2 or 3 points larger than the main text. They can be printed in bold type, or bold italic type, and, if you prefer, they can have a horizontal rule running above them. If you place a horizontal rule BENEATH a subheading it tends to alienate the subheading from its paragraph.

One thing you should remember is to leave more space above a subheading than below it, thus emphasizing the relationship of the subheading to the paragraph that follows it.

Sub-subheadings. A subheading item can have its own subdivision with a *sub-subheading.* If you have more than two levels of divisions it may be less confusing if you refer to them as *heading, A-level subheading, B-level subheading,* etc. Each one of these requires its own style and size of typeface and, possibly, its own degree of paragraph indentation.

For this book I use a *lead-in* sub-subheading as you can see in the paragraph above this one. It is set in the same point size as the rest of the paragraph, except it is boldface italic.

Lonely subheadings

A subheading appearing near the bottom of a page or column should be followed by at least two lines of text.

Since we are now talking about an area larger than one line of type you need to be more skillful than when dealing with word-breaks. Try the trick of adding or subtracting words in nearby paragraphs. Try resetting these nearby paragraphs with more, or less, space.

If these techniques do not work without creating other problems (e.g., open or close lines), then resort to the following emergency-only tactic: Add an extra line of text to the page. I know I said on page 3:16 that the text area on all complete pages should be the same depth, but this may be one of those occasions when you have to break the rule. If you do, you should camouflage the move by adding an extra line to the page facing it so that the visual effect of the spread is not compromised.

House style guide

In addition to maintaining a consistent look to the layout of your book, it is crucial that you maintain a consistency in such less obvious areas as spelling, punctuation, and emphasis.

If one of the large publishing houses accepts your manuscript they will send you an author's manual explaining the way they will produce your book, and how you can help in the process. The manual will include a section on the *house style*, listing the specific way they abbreviate (e.g., NBC not N.B.C., but U.S. not US), how they refer to dates (e.g., the twentieth century, not 20th century), and their particular choice of spelling. They may tell you, for example, that they use a particular edition of a Merriam-Webster dictionary and that, if there is a choice of spelling, they select the first one listed.

These house manuals also indicate which of the major style books they use, advising you to use the same one (e.g., *The Chicago Manual of Style, U.S. Government Printing Office Style Manual, New York Times Manual of Style and Usage,* etc.).

As a publisher you should have your own house style guide in addition to a good dictionary and one of these major style books, particularly if you intend to publish more than one book. Remember, there are occasions when these other style books list more than one way of doing something, and it is up to you to decide which way YOU want to do it.

Your house style guide can also serve as an instant reminder for the spelling of certain words you use regularly: For example, are "bookstore," "cookbook," "proofreading" written as one or two words? What about "front matter," and "page makeup"? Be specific: As a noun "pasteup" is one word but as a verb it is two words ("paste up"), for example.

Consistency is important.   Be consistent in the way you emphasize words. For example, in this book when I use technical terms for the first time I set them in italics, and when I want to add stress to words I use small caps. In this way I make a distinction between the two forms of emphasis. When I need to use certain words to illustrate a point, I enclose them in quotation marks, as you can see in the previous paragraph.

If you do not have a note of these vagaries of style you

may forget which is which. Give copies of your style guide to your editor and your typesetter to avoid unnecessary misunderstandings later.

Keep an eye open for a second-hand copy of one of those publisher in-house style manuals; it can be invaluable to your own publishing house.

One respected and not-too-expensive dictionary is *Webster's Ninth New Collegiate Dictionary*, published by Merriam-Webster. Another style book is *Webster's Standard American Style Manual*, available from the same publisher.

Word processing and desktop publishing programs also have *style sheets*, although they are not the same as what I am talking about here. On the computer a style sheet usually identifies specific type sizes, margin widths, and page layouts for a particular document or book. Different documents and books can have different style sheets. But with a *publishing house style guide* the standards are intended for all publications produced by that house and, consequently, they should be kept separate from word processing or desktop publishing style sheets.

Below: Two standard sheets of paper used for books — 25" x 38" and 23" x 35".

Right: The 23" x 35" sheet is divided into a 16-page signature. When the pages are first printed on this sheet they appear in a strange sequence: page 1 is on the front next to page 16, while page 2 is on the back next to page 15. But when the sheet is folded and trimmed, the pages fall into a logical sequence.

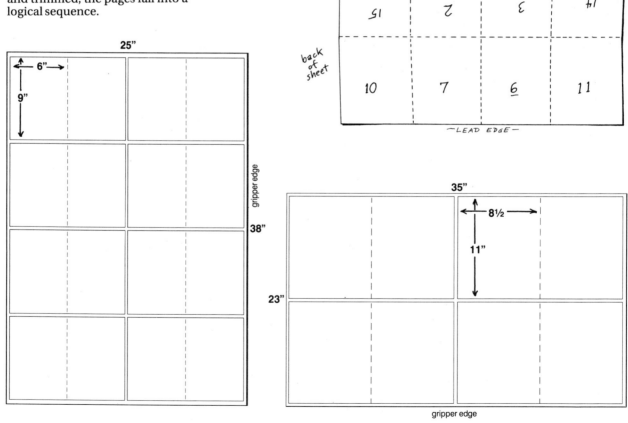

10

How many pages?

Most books are printed on large sheets of paper which are then folded into sections consisting of either 8, 16, or 32 pages. Each of these sections is a *signature* — a term dating back to the days when a printer would sign his or her name after checking the position of pages on the sheet.

When the sheet is first printed the pages appear in a strange sequence with no apparent order. But when the sheet is folded and the edges are trimmed the pages fall into a logical sequence. This positioning of the pages is called *imposition*.

The two standard sheets of paper used for books are 25" x 38" and 23" x 35". The printer will decide which one is more appropriate according to the trim size of your book. As you see in the illustration, if your book is 6" x 9" the 25" x 38" sheet will yield either 1 32-page signature, 2 16-page signatures, 4 8-page signatures, or 8 4-page signatures. The 23" x 35" sheet is more suited to the 8½" x 11" book, and can give you either 1 16-page signature, 2 8-page signatures, or 4 4-page signatures.

For greater economy, most books are printed with either 32-page signatures or 16-page signatures, and you should plan your book to utilize one of these combinations. A book with 32-page signatures can have, say, 128, 160, 192, 224, 256, or 288 pages, and so on.

The cast-off
The number of pages you'll need for the book will depend first of all on the length of the manuscript.

The number of words that can be printed on each page will depend on the style and size of type being used, the amount of leading you insert, and the amount of space you have allocated for the text.

Assuming you have selected a typeface, you can now determine how many pages your book will need. But to count the actual words will not help because the words will be of different lengths.

So, daunting though it may sound at first, you have to count every *character* (letter, number, punctuation mark, and space). Once you have this figure you can determine how many characters will fit on each page when using such-and-such a typeface. This process is called a *cast-off.*

There are two ways of doing a cast-off:

- You decide how many pages the book will have, and then make your manuscript fit.
- You allow the manuscript to occupy as many pages as it wants.

Traditional publishers work with the first method. They determine a budget for the overall cost of producing a book, taking into account the *PPB* (paper, printing and binding), author's royalties, and basic overhead expenses, and then they decide how many pages they can afford if the book is to make a profit.

Small publishers do not incur such high expenses and they can afford to be generous, especially since — for their first book, at least — they are less concerned about making a profit than they are in just publishing it. For them, the second method is more appropriate; also, it requires a lot fewer calculations.

All you really need to know is

- the point size of the typeface you are using
- how much leading you need
- the size of the columns of text.

Assuming your book is a straightforward text, you can hand the manuscript to a typesetter and wait until you get the proofs before determining the number of pages.

Or, you can ask the typesetter to do the calculations for you beforehand.

The remainder of this chapter explains the traditional methods of casting off and copyfitting.

Counting characters in a manuscript

There are several ways to count the characters in a typed manuscript, all of which assume that the manuscript has been typed evenly, with all pages (except, maybe, chapter endings) having the same number of lines and with margins that are the same on all pages.

One way is to count the number of characters on an average line, multiply it by the number of lines on each page, and multiply that figure by the number of pages.

To find the average line, rule a pencil line down the page at the end of the longest line, another at the end of the shortest (not counting very short lines that end paragraphs), and a third half-way between these two.

Count the characters (remember to include punctuation marks and spaces) between the left-hand edge of the type area and this middle line, and then multiply that sum by the number of lines on the page.

Allow for short pages. If you have several pages with less than half the text (such as chapter endings), you should figure how many complete pages they would make if added together, even if you arbitrarily decide that two half-pages will make up one page, or three one-third-pages will make up one page.

There is another way of counting characters, if you have a typewriter that has either pica or elite type. Pica type will give you 10 characters to the inch, and elite will give you 12. Measure an average line, and then multiply it by either 10 or 12 to get the number of characters on each line.

If you have one of those typewriters that use daisy-wheels or typeballs with proportionally spaced characters, you should use a ruler to determine the average number of characters per inch.

None of these methods can be used on manuscripts typed with *justified* lines.

Calculate extracts separately. If your manuscript has been typed on a computer then all configurations will be taken care of for you. However, these methods work only for the main body of text. If you have extracts you will have to make a separate count for them.

As an example, assume you used an elite typewriter,

and your manuscript lines average 6½". You will have an average of 78 characters on each line (6½ x 12 = 78). On a piece of paper jot down these calculations:

manuscript characters per line	78
times number of lines	x 26
= characters per page	2,028
times number of pages	x 220
= characters in manuscript	446,160

Make a separate note for each different size of type, but do not add the figures together.

characters in extracts   =   6,125

Counting lines in a book

Now that we know how many characters are in the manuscript, we need to see how many lines (and, subsequently, how many pages) you will need for the text. This is referred to as *copyfitting*.

To get a truly accurate configuation you have to use a table provided by the people who will be setting the type for you, because there can be subtle shifts in the size of the type depending on the machinery or the program they use. More than likely, the table they'll show you will be based on the *alphabet length* of the typeface — that is, the length of the complete alphabet (a-z) when set in lowercase, and measured in either points or picas.

For an example, we can assume you are going to use 10-point Baskerville with 1-point leading (10/11) as a block approximately 4¼" x 7" on a 6" x 9" page.

Typesetters refer to the length of a line of type as a *measure*, and they define it in picas. They define the depth of a block of text by the number of lines in it.

According to a typesetter's sample book, 10-point Baskerville has an alphabet length of 124 points.

You then look at a table which indicates how many 10-point Baskerville characters will fit on specific measures. It will look something like this:

	1	10	12	14	16	18	20	22	24	26	28	30	32	34	36	38	40	42	Picas
Alphabet Length 124	2.70	27	32	38	43	49	54	59	65	70	76	81	86	92	97	103	108	113	

The bold numbers on the upper line represent various measures from 1 pica to 42 picas. If we look under the 26-pica measure we see that you will have 70 characters on each line of text. This table is known as a *CPP table* (characters per pica). As you can see from the first column, there are 2.70 characters per pica.

We now know we get 70 characters on each line. To determine the number of lines on each page we use the combined measurement of typeface plus leading (in this case, 11 points). You want your block of text to be 7" deep. If you hold the Haberule against an inch ruler you will see you get 46 11-point lines of type in 7".

Bringing the two together

Multiply 70 characters by 46 lines and you get 3,220 characters on each page. On your piece of paper you can now do a few more calculations:

typeset characters per line	70
times number of lines	x 46
= characters per page	3,220

Divide the number of characters in the manuscript (446,160) by the number of typeset characters per page (3,220) and you get 138½ pages.

If you set your extracts in 9/10 Baskerville on an indented measure of 22 picas, you will get 3,300 characters per page. So allow two more pages for your 6,125 extract characters.

Now the other pages

In addition to the pages of text, you have several other pages that must be accounted for. The next chapter deals with these in greater detail, but for the benefit of this example let us assume you decide on the following combination:

number of pages for main text	139
number of pages for extracts	2
front matter pages	17
back matter pages	13
section titles; blank verso pages	6
pages of photos or illustrations	15
Total	192

192 pages divided by 32 = 6 signatures

Rarely will it round out to an even number of signatures this easily without a few adjustments. If, for example, you came up with only 189 pages, you could still print your book with 192 pages and leave the three extra pages blank. If that seems a waste, you could be creative and add a note about the author (if you do not have a similar note already) or an advertisement for your next book.

But if you have, say, 195 pages you should go through and see where you can cut out three pages. Maybe you can close up your back matter, or not be so generous with the blank verso pages. Maybe you can set the index in narrower columns, requiring fewer pages.

What if you have 216 pages, and you cannot cut 24, nor do you want to add another 8 to make up seven signatures (224 pages)? Most printers can print your book with six 32-page signatures, adding one with 16 pages and another with 8 pages, but you will pay slightly more than if it were an even number of 32-page signatures. Costs mount as the combination of signature sizes becomes more complex.

If you are intimidated by the mathematics of a cast-off, you can leave the configurations to your typesetter, who is more familiar with the process.

11

Some specific pages

Traditionally, non-fiction books consist of three parts: front matter, text, and back matter. Front matter is also called *preliminaries* or *prelims*. If there is one aspect of book design that separates the big guys (i.e., the established publishing houses) from the little ones it is the way these parts are handled. Over many years a certain formula has evolved — one that may seem stodgy, but that nonetheless is very practical. As in any other field, there are rules the players should know before they break them. Although there may be slight deviations, the basic sequence of pages should be:

FRONT MATTER:
Endpaper (hardcover book only)
Blank leaf
Bastard title (or half title)
Frontispiece
Title page
Copyright page
Dedication
Acknowledgments
Foreword
Preface
Table of contents
List of illustrations
Introduction

TEXT:
Half title (or part title)
Text, in chapters

BACK MATTER:
Notes
Bibliography
Glossary
Index
Colophon
Blank leaf, or leaves
Endpaper (hardcover book only)

Endpaper

If the book is a hardcover, the first page we see when opening it is the *endpaper* — also called *end leaf,* or *end sheet.* This is of a heavier paper than the pages of the book because it has to support the cover board as well as the bulk of the book.

A touch of elegance can be achieved here by using a colored sheet that will match or complement the dominant color appearing on the jacket. You could also fill this otherwise blank area with a map or some other suitable illustration. Paperback books do not have endpapers.

Blank leaf

In a hardcover book, this is the page immediately after the endpaper. It is usually attached to the endpaper with a thin strip of glue.

In a paperback, it is the first sheet we see when opening the book.

Today, the name *blank leaf i*s a misnomer since this page is rarely blank. Traditionally, however, it was void of type or graphics. Adrian Wilson, one of California's finest letterpress printers and book designers, said the blank leaf provides "a moment of rest and anticipation after the force of the jacket or binding and before the usually subdued announcement in the bastard title of what is to come." For me, it has an added *raison d'etre:* It enables the paper itself to take a bow, rather like a musician before a performance.

You might also consider this page the private territory of the book's eventual owner, since very often it is the page on which a greeting or simply the owner's name will be written.

To some publishers, leaving a whole page blank may seem a waste of paper and money. But blank pages are just as vital to a book's design as are other elements, and allowances should be made for them. If you have to put something here, keep it brief: a short quotation, or a small piece of ornamentation, for example. For me, a block of text on this first page has a jarring effect, denying me that "moment of rest and anticipation."

Although a page number will rarely appear here, this should be counted as the first page of the book.

Bastard title (or, half title)

In olden times books were printed and sold without covers, and the buyers would have them bound in a style appropriate for their own libraries. The title page, which was often elaborately adorned with splendid ornamentation, was the third page. The words of the title were repeated on the first page to help identify that particular stack of unbound pages, and in time this became known as the *bastard title*, as opposed to the legitimate title. In many cases the bastard title page was later discarded, and was not bound in the book.

Today, a book's title often appears on a page of its own in the very beginning of the book. It is still called the bastard title, although it is sometimes also referred to as a *half title*. If a book is broken into several sections, each section has its own half title, so there is a certain wisdom in retaining the designation *bastard title* when referring to this specific page at the front of the book.

Because of its importance, the bastard title must appear on a right-hand page. And, as with all the half-title pages, the wording on this page should be kept to a minimum. It should be the title of the book, either with or without the sub-title. It can be placed in exactly the same position it occupies on the title page (and in the same typeface), or it can align with the half titles of the different sections found elsewhere in the book.

Position is important. Usually the bastard title is either centered across the page, or it is *flush right* (that is, with the last word of each line aligned with the right edge of the text area). If placed on the left of the page, it will be overpowered by the mass of white space to the right, rather than being in command of the page.

Although steeped in tradition, the bastard title is no longer considered essential, and it can be given up if necessary. But allow for it anyway. You can delete it later IF you find you are short of pages. But not yet. It adds a touch of elegance, and it should be retained if possible. However, its inclusion could be pretentious if there is not much in the front matter other than, say, the title and copyright pages.

Author's signature

The question of where and how an author signs a book is rarely considered when a book is designed, yet it can become a delicate issue when people start clamoring for an autographed copy. Since that author may be you, let's take a side trip and discuss the issue now.

Many people, especially if they are writing a message of some sort with their signature, will use the bastard title page where there is always plenty of room; also, the book's title is there as identification. Others scrawl a message over and around the type on the title page, disregarding the designer's efforts in laying out that page (imagine an artist signing a painting in that manner!).

Then there are those who sign the first blank page in the book. This is probably the least appropriate place since there is no printed connection with the author's name. Anyway, as suggested above, that page belongs to the book's owner and usually carries the inscription of Aunt Emma, or whoever the benefactor was.

The title page is better because there is a direct link with the author. An author with a sense of design will instinctively inscribe a title page so that the inscription becomes another element of the design.

But the bastard title page is appropriate since it has a lot of white space as well as the book's title.

Looking ahead. The issue is not a trivial one, particularly if you look ahead to the day when your book might become a collector's item. Even if it never becomes so prized, at least there is a chance it will turn up in a second-hand bookstore sooner or later. When it does, the value of the copy will depend on several factors unrelated to the physical condition of the book. Collectors and second-hand book dealers use terms such as *dedication, inscribed, presentation* and *signed*.

- A *dedication* copy is one in which the author has written an inscription for the person to whom the book is dedicated.
- An *inscribed* copy is one in which the author has written an inscription to a specific person.
- When an author gives a copy to someone who helped in some way with the book, and this is indicated in the inscription ("To Mary, with grateful thanks for your help in gathering this material," for example), it becomes a *presentation* copy.
- A book bearing only the signature is a *signed* copy.

Of the four, the dedication copy is possibly the most

valued since there is likely to be only one like it. Next in value would be the presentation copy.

A book inscribed to some unknown or unrelated person is likely to be priced lower than one bearing only the signature of the author. Imagine yourself in a second-hand bookstore where three copies of the same book are available. One is inscribed to an unknown person, one bears only the author's signature, and one is not signed at all. Assuming all are in good condition, and the prices are comparable, which one would you buy to display on your shelf and to show to your friends? My bet is you would choose the one with the author's signature alone.

How to sign a book. Despite this, however, we should not deny the great personal value and sense of pride felt by the original recipient of an inscribed book. For many of us, such an opportunity is rare, and we treasure it.

Robert A. Wilson, in his *Modern Book Collecting* (Alfred A. Knopf, 1980), says that some authors are very particular how they inscribe books, and they try to clarify the relationship between signer and signee. Wilson writes:

> T.S. Eliot, when making an actual presentation to a friend, would write 'For —— from T.S. Eliot'; when asked by a stranger to sign or inscribe a book, he would write 'Inscribed for —— by T.S. Eliot'.

While on this topic, it is appropriate to warn against one of the greatest enemies of book permanence — the ballpoint pen. Not only do these pens tend to dig deep into the paper, creating burrows on the underlying pages, but the ink in time spreads and creates ugly blotches which may bleed through to other pages. A regular ink pen, with fine point, should be used.

Frontispiece

Originally, a *frontispiece* was an illustration facing the title page, although today the term is often used to define the page itself rather than what is on it.

Because the title page is always a right-hand page, the frontispiece page always falls on the left. You can put either a photograph or line drawing here, or you can spread out the display type from the title page. You can also leave it blank (preferable), although there is a tendency — particularly if the author is famous — to

The Last
Wilderness

600 miles by canoe and portage in the Northwest Territories

Peter Browning

GREAT WEST BOOKS   LAFAYETTE, CALIFORNIA

HARVEST

Jean Giono

Translated by Henri Fluchère and Geoffrey Myers

NORTH POINT PRESS · SAN FRANCISCO
1983

THE EARTH MANUAL

How to Work on Wild Land
Without Taming It

by Malcolm Margolin

Drawings by Michael Harney

HEYDAY BOOKS, BERKELEY

Notes
from a
Bottle
Found
on the
Beach
at
Carmel

Evan S. Connell

1984
North Point Press · San Francisco

Four title pages, each illustrating a skillful arrangement of different weights and sizes of type.

place the *advertisement card* (list of the author's other books) here. Whatever you do with this page, remember that of all the two-page spreads in the book this is the most critical, and the frontispiece and the title page must work in harmony with each other.

Do not let a heavy photograph overpower the title page.

Title page

The title page is the most significant page of a book. It establishes the overall tone without resorting to the hard-sell trappings deemed so essential to the cover, and it is the chief source of bibliographic information for the *Anglo-American Cataloging Rules*, the guidelines by which libraries catalog books. Approach its design with respect.

Because of its importance, it should always be a right-hand page although, as already indicated, it can spread across the frontispiece. Words should be kept to a minimum yet provide the following data: title, sub-title, author, name of publisher, and city where published. The Library of Congress specifies that a book must have on its title page a U.S. city as place of publication or it will not be assigned a catalog card number (LCCN).

➤ *See LCCN, pages 12:102–3.*

If illustrators or translators are involved, their names should appear here, as should the name of the editor in the case of an edited anthology.

When appropriate, indicate whether this is a revised edition, or second edition, etc. Do not confuse the term *new edition*, which includes additional and amended copy, with *new printing*, which simply refers to a re-printing of the same edition without corrections.

Many publishers include the year of first publication.

If your company has a logo you could place it on this page. You could also include an illustration or symbol pertaining to the book.

Choice of type. But the most important element of all, as far as the design is concerned, will be the typeface. This display type should match or complement the display type used for chapter titles.

To distinguish the relative importance of each item you

can vary the point size of type and also select different weights (bold, semi-bold, italic, small caps, etc.). The title could be set in a custom hand-drawn face, in dramatic contrast to the other type yet still appropriate to the book's theme. Remember: A good contrast is better than a poor match.

Do not make the mistake of assuming that the title page and the cover are interchangeable, or — worse yet — that they are the same. Each has its own function. The cover invites someone to pick up the book, often employing techniques used in billboards and magazine advertisements, while the title page presents the basic facts with more subtlety and finesse, at the same time hinting at what is to come.

Despite this difference, there should be a common thread between the two designs. All too often a cover design will bear no relationship whatever to the title page or to the rest of the book. This is usually because two different people were given the assignments, and no provision was made to link them in any way. A good tie-in, or bridge, will be the way the title is presented. Ideally, on both the cover and the title page it should be in the same typeface, placed in the same position (centered, or flush right, for example).

There is a temptation to take the same blocks of type used on the cover and repeat them on the title page. If you do this, consider reducing them slightly or you will find our old enemy optical illusion wreaking havoc. On the cover the words may be printed in a light color; inside the book they are printed in a solid black, causing them to appear larger and more overpowering. Conversely, that heavy type can appear hemmed in by its position on an inside page.

Symmetrical or asymmetrical? You need to decide whether the title page will be symmetrical or asymmetrical. Will all lines of type be centered, or carefully set apart from each other to create a certain graphics effect? You can select different sizes of type according to the relative importance of each line, as long as they are harmonious with one another.

If you use a photograph or other form of illustration, remember that it too has a visual weight that needs to be balanced with the weight of the words. And be mindful of what is happening to the white space when you position all these different elements, since the space itself is one of your design elements.

Use as a guide the layout formula you designed for the main pages of text (text area, margins, etc.). Alternatively, you could come up with a layout for the title page that bears no relation at all to the other pages, yet somehow retains the flavor of the book. In other words, there are safe guidelines to work within, but there is also plenty of room for creativity.

Avoid zigzag. If you are going to run illustrations or type across the title page spread, watch out for the *gutter* that separates the pages. Depending on how thick the book will be, a certain amount of space will be hidden in the fold, and the result could be disastrous if not planned for. Normally you need at least ⅝" margin on the inner edge of each page to allow for this.

Be aware also that if you have a straight line (whether as type or part of the illustration) cutting across the gutter it will appear to zigzag if the two pages are not aligned perfectly when bound together. Since you will have no control over the binding of the book, you should play safe and not tempt fate.

Repeating the body text area. In designing the title page for *Bummer & Lazarus* I kept all elements within the same area as the body text. Although the larger lines of type ran across the entire area, I maintained the two-column effect with my positioning of the illustration and the names of author and illustrator.

Originally I had wanted to include the Londonborn Publications logo (Tower Bridge within an egg) on the title page. I had cut-outs of each element and toyed with them on a sheet of paper, moving them around in an effort to fit them all on the same page. The obvious place for the logo was on the same line as Londonborn Publications, but to put it there I would have had to reduce the type. To put it on its own would have disturbed the balance of the other elements. Finally I put it by itself on the opposite page. But even then I placed it so that it would line up and be in harmony with the various elements on the title page. Visually, the two pages now work as one.

Sadly, on the first printing of the book (paperback and hardcover) the title page slipped, so that it ended up with the wider margin at the top, throwing the whole thing out of alignment with the rest of the book. This is something I should have noticed when proofing the *blueline* (the printer's final proof) and corrected before the presses ran, but I did not. I corrected it on the second printing, but I still shudder when I see that first printing. I tell you this so that you may learn from my mistake: Check, and re-check, everything before it is too late.

For the main title I used Chisel, which seemed to be appropriate for the period, besides being suggestive of the playfulness of the two dogs. The subtitle and other lines were set in different sizes of either Bold Latin or Wide Latin which have similarly pointed serifs and wide letters. Bold Latin was also used for major headings throughout the book.

➤ *See Chapter 17 (**The cover design**) when considering the design of the title page.*

12

Copyright page

This entire chapter is devoted to the odd assortment of elements sometimes found on the copyright page.

The Copyright Act of 1909 specified that the copyright notice for a book had to appear either on the title page or on the page immediately following it. Most publishers chose the latter, placing it on the reverse of the title page, thus establishing a tradition that continues today even though the Act of 1976 makes no such demands, other than that the notice "shall be affixed to the copies in such manner and location as to give reasonable notice of the claim of copyright" (Section 401(c)).

This page has become a repository of miscellaneous information, most of which is vital to the book's credibility but is rarely looked at by the average reader. Here are elements that are not directly related to the book's subject matter but that must be included. Each requires its own specific treatment.

Librarians refer to this page for Cataloging in Publication Data (CIP), which tells them how to categorize the book. By looking at the date your book was copyrighted and when it was last printed researchers can determine how current or how dated your materials and/or opinions might be. And if your readers want to know the address of the publisher, this is the page where they expect to find it.

This page may seem like the junk drawer we all have, in which we toss everything we cannot find another place for, but its design requires as much attention as any other page in the book.

When Steve Renick, Design Director of the University of California Press, Berkeley, judges a book's design this is the first page he looks at. He says he holds the designer accountable for the information on that page, and he adds that it has to be completely integrated in the overall design of the book.

Usually the type here is considerably smaller than that on the text pages, although it must still be easy to read. Either 8-point or 9-point type is adequate. Sometimes, if there is not too much data, it is set in italics.

Copyright notice

There are two major international copyright treaties: The Universal Copyright Convention (UCC) to which the U.S. became a signatory in 1952, and the older and more prestigious Berne Union for the Protection of Literary and Artistic Property (Berne Convention) which came into effect in 1886. The U.S. did not sign the Berne Convention because it would have meant making drastic changes in the way copyright was applied in this country. But, on November 1, 1988, after heated debates in both houses of Congress, legislation was signed by President Reagan enabling the U.S. to join. As a result, the copyright laws of this country changed.

The most significant change is that a work (book, story, sculpture, etc.) published since March 1, 1989, does not have to have a copyright notice attached in order to be protected. It is protected automatically under the international law.

However, you'd still be wise to print the familiar copyright symbol in any book you publish because it could prevent misunderstanding. Nobody can say they didn't know it was copyrighted, and you'd have little problem bringing suit against anyone who tried.

Another issue in the house debates was the question of registering copyright. The Library of Congress builds its collection from books submitted by publishers when they register copyright. Since the Berne Convention does not require this registration some people feared that the Library would suffer. Eventually a compromise was reached: Only books produced in the U.S. need now be registered, although even this is not obligatory. As an inducement, publishers registering copyright with the Library of Congress will be given greater consideration and increased statutory damages if they ever become involved in litigation over infringement of copyright. I'll come back to the question of registration later in this chapter.

The generally accepted form of copyright notice is:

© 1990 John Doe. All rights reserved.

The first part (© 1990 John Doe) is what the 1976 Copyright Act required. The second part (All rights reserved) is required in certain Latin American countries.

Many publishers add something similar to:

No portion of this book may be reproduced or used in any form, or by any means, without prior written permission of the publishers.

On one level they are saying, "Write to us first, and we will consider your request," and on another they are emphasizing that they mean business and will go after violators. Very often if you want to quote something from their book you can get permission to do so, but first they want to be sure you are not extracting too much, to the detriment of their publication. They also want to ensure that you give them proper credit, and that the quote is not used in a derogatory way. They may even want to be paid.

Now that you are a publisher you will find yourself on the other side of the fence. You should prepare yourself for such an eventuality and include a similar notice on your copyright page.

If you publish updated editions of your book, with supplementary or corrected material, you could add separate copyright notices indicating the years of amendment. In effect, you are now copyrighting the new material being added. Remember that a straight reprint, without major corrections to the contents, is referred to as an additional *printing*, not a new edition, and it will not require a new copyright notice. One way would be to add the dates as they occur:

© 1990, 1992, 1993 John Doe. All rights reserved.

Separate copyright notices. The writer, as well as any illustrator or photographer involved with a book, should copyright his or her own work. Separate notices for each person should be included on the copyright page. Copyright cannot be obtained in the name of the publisher unless the author transfers the rights to the publisher. According to the act, the term "authors" includes writers, illustrators, sculptors, and any other originators of work.

Registering your copyright. If you are the author and the publisher you should copyright the work in your own name rather than in the name of your publishing house. One reason is that if you later sell the business, along with all titles you have published (whether they are your own or someone else's), at least you can hang on to the copyright.

In order to register your copyright write to Washington and ask for the appropriate form. Then fill it out and return it with a check for $10 and "two complete copies of the best edition" of the book. By "best edition" they mean that if you publish a paperback and a hardcover simultaneously, then you should submit two copies of the hardcover.

If the book is mainly text (fiction or non-fiction), you should apply for Form TX (for text). If it is a book primarily of photographs or art work, then you ask for Form VA (for visual arts). Write to:

> Copyright Office
> Library of Congress
> Washington, D.C. 20559

At the same time you might as well ask for a copy of the Copyright Act of 1976. Now that you are a bona fide publisher you need to be aware of some of the subtleties of this very important law.

Publishing history

Somewhere close to your copyright notice you can include details about when the book was first published and how many printings you have had. Even though you are still working on the first printing, you need to plan ahead if you want to avoid redesigning the page later on. Any of the following styles is valid:

> First printed March 1990
> Published March 1990
> First printed 1990
> Published 1990

You add subsequent printing dates as they occur.

Another way, one that will not require any new type being set, is to use a row of descending numbers. The first printing would look like this:

> 10 9 8 7 6 5 4 3 2 1

The lowest number represents that particular printing. For the second printing you will simply delete the 1, for the third you will delete the 2, and so forth.

Country where manufactured

Books printed outside the United States and Canada before July 1, 1986, ran into several complications under the Manufacturing Clause of the Copyright Act. Unless the books complied with certain limitations they were denied copyright protection in the United States and it became necessary to print a notice in each book stating where the book was manufactured. That is why you will see the words

Printed in the United States of America

on either the title page or the copyright page of books printed in this country prior to that date. Books printed overseas usually have a similar notice, as for example,

Printed in Japan.

Although the Manufacturing Clause expired on July 1, 1986, you may still see a reference to where newer books are printed, probably in deference to the customs authorities of countries to which the book may be exported. So go ahead and put it in your book. Sometimes the word "Manufactured" is used instead of "Printed," emphasizing that ALL the work is done in that country, not just the printing.

CIP data

To help libraries categorize new books, the Library of Congress preassigns cataloging information through a program called Cataloging in Publication (CIP). This information is sent to publishers who then print it on the copyright page.

In order to participate in the CIP program you should write to:

Library of Congress
Cataloging in Publication Division
Washington, D.C. 20540

and ask for a Publisher's Response Form. If after submitting this form you are accepted into the program you will be sent another form which has to be submitted with "a full galley or typewritten copy of the book." If you cannot do this, you should send "a facsimile of the title page and copyright page" along with other items such as table of contents, index, in-house abstract or summary, and sample chapters.

Based on that material, the Library will assign your book certain numbers and categories which will be printed on a card and sent to you with instructions to reprint them on the copyright page of your book exactly as they are printed on the card.

Look at the adjoining illustration as an example of what is included in the CIP data. This is for a book of quotations of naturalist John Muir.

The numbers are: Library of Congress classification number, Dewey Decimal number, Library of Congress catalog card number, and the ISBN. The various headings will be repeated in the card catalog file of any library carrying the book.

The abbreviation "alk. paper" indicates that the book is printed on alkaline paper — i.e., an acid-free paper. I'll go into greater detail on this in Chapter 23.

Even though the Library of Congress asks that the information be printed exactly as printed on their card, some designers take the liberty of changing the bold typeface indicated for the one line "Library of Congress Cataloging in Publication Data" because it tends to upset the weight of the type on that page if everything else has been set in light faces.

The CIP manual states that "all monographic trade publications published in the United States" are within the scope of the CIP program, although it goes on to delineate 14 categories that are not eligible. There, amongst telephone directories, coloring books, and religious instructional material are "books paid for or subsidized by individual authors; books published by a house which publishes only the works of one author."

This has not deterred several self-publishers from submitting their books, many of which were subsequently accepted into the program.

Library of Congress Cataloging-in-Publication Data

Muir, John, 1838–1914.
    John Muir in his own words.

    Includes index.
    1. Muir, John, 1838–1914. 2. Natural history—United States. 3. Nature conservation—United States. 4. Naturalists—United States—Biography. I. Browning, Peter, 1928–   . II. Title.
QH31.M9A3 1988   508.794   87–83325
ISBN 0–944220–02–9 (pbk. : alk. paper)

The numbers appearing on this CIP data card are: Library of Congress classification (QH31.M9A3 1988); Dewey Decimal classification (508.794); Library of Congress classification (87-83325); ISBN (0-944220-02-9).

LCCN

If you do not qualify for the CIP program you can still apply for and receive a Library of Congress Catalog Card Number (LCCN). To apply for one, write to the same address as for CIP (see previous page), but in your letter ask for a "Request for Preassignment of Library of Congress Catalog Card Number."

Based on the information you supply on the form, the Library will issue you a number which you print on the copyright page. It will look something like this:

Library of Congress Catalog Card Number: 89-12345

The first two digits indicate the year in which the card number was assigned, which may not be the same as the year in which the book is published.

However, just because a number is assigned does not mean the book will end up in the catalog of the Library of Congress. It is merely the preliminary step. As soon as you receive your books from the printer you should send a complimentary copy to the Library, using their postage-free label. The book will undergo a final review in its published form by the Library staff before the big decision is made.

You should not delay in sending a copy. The cataloging procedure cannot be completed until the Libary of Congress gets your book, and until then the Library cannot begin printing cards for libraries around the world.

Only books that list on their title page a U.S. city as place of production are included in this program.

ISBN

International Standard Book Numbering is based on a system first introduced in the United Kingdom in 1967 and is intended to help bookstores around the world keep track of their inventories. In addition to the international administration agency, based in Berlin, there are a number of national agencies. R.R. Bowker in New York acts as the agency for the United States, and it is to them that you should write for your own set of numbers and Users' Manual. The address is:

International Standard Book Number Agency
R.R. Bowker
245 West 17th Street
New York, N.Y. 10011

The International Standard Book Number (ISBN) is crucial if you intend to market your book through bookstores. You probably have noticed when buying books that the sales clerk invariably turns a book over to look at the numbers printed in the lower right-hand corner of the back cover. By punching that number (ISBN) into the store's computer the clerk can adjust the inventory as well as register the sale.

There are literally tens of thousands of those ISBNs in use around the world, all with only ten digits, yet there are no two alike. Each one can be used to trace the publisher and a particular book.

For this book the ISBN is:

0-930235-08-8

The ten-digit number is broken into four parts, each part called an *identifier*. The first part identifies the national, geographic, or language grouping of the publisher; the second identifies the publisher; the third (in combination with the fourth) identifies the book; and the fourth is a single digit that provides an automatic check on the correctness of the ISBN.

All English-language publishers have ISBNs beginning with 0. Other examples are: 2 for French-language publishers, 3 for German-language publishers, and 5 for Russian-language publishers.

Bowker will send you an *ISBN Log Book* — a list of numbers all beginning with the same two identifiers. The third and fourth identifiers in each number will vary, and it is up to you to assign one specific combination to each separate edition.

Each book that you publish must have a separate ISBN. Also, each edition must have a separate number. In other words, if you print a paperback edition and a hardcover edition of the same title, each must have its own number. Then, if you later publish an updated edition, with major corrections and amendments, it too must be given a different number.

The ISBN Users' Manual specifies that, in the case of books, the number must appear whenever possible:

On the reverse of the title page, or, if this is not possible, on the base of the title page, or, if this too is not possible, at some other conspicuous location in the book.
On the base of the spine.
On the back of the cover in nine-point type or larger.

On the back of the dust-jacket, and on the back of
any other protective case or wrapper.
The ISBN should always be printed in type large
enough to be easily legible (e.g. not smaller than
9 point).

Advance Book Information

The Advance Book Information has nothing to do with
book design, but it will play an essential part in marketing your book. When applying for the LCCN and ISBN
forms you could deal also with the ABI. Write to:

R.R. Bowker
Books in Print Dept.
245 West 17th Street
New York, N.Y. 10011

and ask for an ABI form. The information you supply on
this form will be reprinted in a number of books used
extensively in the book trade, including the *Books in
Print* series which is constantly referred to by bookstore people. All it costs you is the postage.

Acid-free paper

If you print your book on acid-free paper you can include the following compliance notice on the copyright
page as recommended by The American National
Standards Institute, Inc., in 1984:

 The paper used in this publication meets the minimum requirements of American National Standard
for Information Sciences — Permanence of Paper
for Printed Library Materials, ANSI Z39.48-1984.

Also, as you saw illustrated on page 12:102, the Library
of Congress will include a reference in the CIP data.

➤   *See Chapter 23 for more about acid-free paper.*

Credits and permissions

Unless you are listing them with the acknowledgments,
you may want to include on this page the credits for
photographs, illustrations, or lengthy quotations from
other sources.

Colophon

The word *colophon* once had a very specific meaning,
but today it is less precise. Originally, it consisted of the
trademark, or signature, of a printer-publisher at a

Library of Congress Cataloging-in-Publication Data

Browning, Peter, 1928–
    The last wilderness : 600 miles by canoe and portage in the
Northwest Territories / Peter Browning. — 2nd ed.
        p.   cm.
    Bibliography: p.
    ISBN 0-944220-03-7 (alk. paper)
    1. Great Slave Lake Region (N.W.T.)—Description and travel.
2. Mackenzie (N.W.T.)—Description and travel. 3. Keewatin
(N.W.T.)—Description and travel. 4. Canoes and canoeing—Northwest
Territories. 5. Browning, Peter, 1928-   —Journeys—Northwest
Territories. 6. Northwest Territories—Description and travel-
–Bibliography. I. Title.
F1100.G8B76 1989
917.19'2—dc19   88-82711
                                                                                  CIP

The illustrations are from woodcuts
by Louis William Graux

Copyright pages for (left) *The Last Wilderness,* Great West Books, and (right) *Harvest,* North Point Press.
See page 13:112 for another approach to copyright page design.

Design by David Bullen
Typeset in Mergenthaler Berkeley Old Style Book and Medium
with Berkeley Old Style Bold display
by Wilsted & Taylor
Printed by Maple-Vail
on acid-free paper

Survival on Montague Island
Book design by David R. Johnson
Cover design, Jackie Pels
Soberg family photos
Typesetting by Archetype, Berkeley, California
Printed and bound at Lompa Press, Albany, California

Hardscratch Press
Walnut Creek, California

All profits from the sale of this book go to the University
of Alaska scholarship fund endowed by the Alaska
Yukon Pioneers, Seattle, Washington.

Colophon pages for (left) *Harvest,* North Point Press, and (right) *Survival on Montague Island,* Hardscratch Press.

time when books were printed and published by the same person or company. The colophon included the printer-publisher's name and address, along with the date, and the patron's name.

When publishers began operating independently, the name and address became known as the *imprint*, and the trademark was called a *colophon*. The term has been stretched to include a list of people who helped with the design and production of the book, together with a list of typefaces, paper stock, etc.

Even the colophon's placement in a book is less precise than it once was. Originally it was the last item in a book, and sometimes it appeared by itself on the very last page. This is in keeping with the meaning of the Greek word, *kolophon:* "summit; finishing touch."

Although some publishers still place the colophon on the last page, most place it on the copyright page; others eliminate it entirely. The publisher's imprint nearly always appears on the title page.

By printing a list of those people who helped with the production of a book a publisher is implying pride in the work done by these individuals. There is also an added bonus: If the typesetters, printers and designers know their contributions to the book will be SIGNED they are more likely to put in that extra effort to ensure it is the best they can do — and what a great portfolio piece it can be for them when they are looking for work!

The information you have in a colophon, whether it is on the copyright page or by itself at the back of the book, can include: names of the typesetter, printer, binder, cover and/or book designer, and the paper and typefaces used.

An important point to remember if you have additional printings is that there may be changes in some of this information. For instance, the paper may be different, either because you realized the first one was unsuitable or because the printer no longer has it in stock. Also, you could have a different binding (instead of Smyth sewn, for instance, you may have it perfect bound), requiring a different binder.

The design of the copyright page
So much for what should, or could, appear on the copyright page. Now for the tricky job of designing it.

As indicated earlier, all of the information should be positioned in such a way that the page remains in harmony with other pages in the book.

The best way is to have all the material set in its final size, then make a photocopy you can cut up and play around with. Move these pieces around beneath the tracing of your master double-spread, and see how they look. Place the page beside mock-ups of other pages to see if it has the same sense of rhythm.

When you have the design you want, paste or tape the pieces to a sheet of paper, and put it aside with the master page layout guide. Do the same with other pages as you come to them, until you have the pattern for all pages that require individual attention.

If there is only a small amount of type it is often better to align everything with the bottom line of the text area of the other pages, leaving the larger area of white space at the top.

Do not mix your typefaces too much (if at all) on this page. Keep the characters small, but still legible: 8-point or 9-point should be adequate.

Remember that this is only one half of a spread. You may want to work on the opposite page before finishing your design for the copyright page.

13

The rest of the front matter

There are still several pages of front matter to consider before we get to the main text.

Dedication
Most books are dedicated to a particular person or a group of people whom the author wishes to honor. It is a very personal message, and yet one that most people will read. It usually has a page of its own somewhere in the front matter. Because of its significance, it is better placed on a right-hand page.

The dedication could be a few words or it could occupy half the page, but in either case you should place it so that it blends with the design of other pages.

Acknowledgments
This is where you thank the people who helped with research and/or production, or who merely offered moral support. In the case of anthologies, this could be where you list all the credits to publishers and writers.

With serious non-fiction most readers assume that the author sought professional help in researching the material and they are curious about where that help came from. By crediting your sources, either here or in your introduction or preface, you are adding credibility to your work.

Again, this is a significant element and requires a right-hand page.

Some publishers are confused by the spelling of the word *acknowledgments*: They are not sure whether to include an *e* after the *g*. The two spellings are offered as alternatives in some American dictionaries, with *acknowledgements* considered the English spelling. Use the first spelling in the dictionary you have chosen as arbiter for the rest of your book.

Front matter text

Foreword, preface, and introduction are three blocks of text usually found in the front matter. Each one has a specific job to do and its own order in the hierarchy. However, there seems to be some confusion as to which is which, and some dictionaries compound the problem by giving all three words (foreword, preface and introduction) the same definition. Even *The Chicago Manual of Style* and Marshall Lee's *Bookmaking* vary in their interpretations.

One popular set of definitions is:

- If you want to tell your readers about YOUR BOOK — how or why you wrote it, etc. — you include a preface.
- If you want to brief them about THE SUBJECT MATTER, then you include an introduction, which will appear as the last item of the preliminaries.
- If the introduction is more an extension of the actual text than a summary, then it is considered part of the text and should appear at the beginning of the main body of text, AFTER the front matter.
- If you include a piece written by someone other than the author, extolling the author's work and credibility, you place it BEFORE all of these other items and call it a foreword.

Foreword

The spelling of the word *foreword* also confuses people, often appearing as *forword* or *forward*. But here you have no choice: There is only one correct way. Think of it as "the *word* that goes be*fore*" (be*fore-word*), since it appears as the first text item in the book.

The foreword is usually written by an authority on the book's topic and is intended as an assurance that the author knows what she or he is writing about. The name of this authority can appear either at the beginning, under the heading, or it can be printed at the end of the piece, whichever you prefer.

You may want to include a few words explaining who

the writer is, listing his or her qualifications pertinent to the book. Often you can boost your book's sales by including this person's name on the cover with wording to the effect of "Foreword by ——."

The foreword should start on a right-hand page. If it is longer than two pages and ends with only a few lines on another right-hand page you should consider cutting the text so that it will end on a left-hand page. This avoids having to leave most of the page blank, followed by another blank page, before the next element can start on a recto page.

Preface

If you, as author, want to include a piece explaining why and how you wrote the book you can place it after the foreword and call it the *preface*. Sometimes this is where authors thank their friends, helpers, and people who gave them moral support, rather than in the earlier *acknowlegments*. It is not a time to discuss the topic of the book at length; that should wait until the *introduction*.

Table of contents

Apart from the copyright page, the hardest page to design is the one on which you list the contents. If you look through a random selection of books you will see there is no standard formula. It may help if you can recall the occasions when you were frustrated trying to find something on the contents page of a book.

Perhaps the chapter title was on the far left and the page number was on the far right, with a chasm as wide as the Grand Canyon separating them. The only way to get from one to the other was to find a straight-edged object to lay on the page. Maybe there was a long row of dots (called *leaders*) spanning the void, which, as you tried to follow with your finger, seemed to sway precariously like one of those rope bridges in jungle movies — and when you made your way to the page indicated, you found you were completely lost because your finger had dropped to a lower "bridge."

Then there are pages with just the opposite effect. There is a profusion of information — titles, subtitles, summaries — all packed tightly on the page in several columns that seem to merge with each other, and you get the feeling the publisher just wanted to get all that information on the page without "wasting" space.

Table of Contents

Contents

Left, the contents page of *The Way We Lived* (Heyday Books) and, right, the contents page of *West of the West* (North Point Press).

Special thanks to Huey Johnson, Dick Raymond, and Life Forum for the grant that made writing this book possible.

Contents

In *The Earth Manual* (Heyday Books) the layout of the contents page echoes that of the copyright page facing it.

But there are contents pages designed so carefully that you can find what you are looking for without any effort. Those are the successful ones. They do their job without any fuss or pretension, and they are the ones to study for ideas in designing this page of your book.

Points to remember:

- A page number should be as close to its title as possible, without being confused as part of the title.
- The type should be easy to read.
- The overall appearance of the page should be in harmony with the rest of the book.

In Chapter 7 I refer to *readability* and *legibility* as the criteria for selecting type. The criterion for your table of contents, as well as for the list of illustrations, and the index, is *findability*. This is especially true in a book such as this one, which is filled with information that the reader may want to refer to constantly. Be as logical as you can when providing the signposts.

If it becomes necessary to use a variety of typefaces and point sizes to help set off different aspects of the contents page, then go ahead and use them, even though they may not be used anywhere else in the book. But the key words are "to help." This should not be an idle excuse to break from the standards you have set for yourself. Nor should this variety of typefaces and sizes contrast greatly with the overall design of your book.

Another exception to the rules would be permissible if the table of contents is two pages long. By starting on the left-hand page and finishing on the right-hand page you can present it in one clean spread, allowing your reader to see the entire spectrum of your book at one glance.

Generally the one word "Contents" is sufficient for the title, rather than "Table of contents."

The words "chapter" and "page" are usually redundant on this page.

If there are only a few items to be listed you could use larger type and center the lines, with the page numbers appearing on a separate line either above or below.

Whichever you choose, it should be obvious to the reader which number belongs to which line.

A lot of people, when deciding whether to buy a book, will study the table of contents to determine what is and isn't included. Think of it as another sales tool.

List of illustrations

The list of illustrations presents a new set of problems. Do you want to list only the titles of the illustrations, or do you want the artist/photogapher/lender's credit along with other pertinent information? Whatever you decide, just remember the basic points:

- The type must be legible.
- The information must be easy to find.
- The page number should be close to the caption or title.
- The whole page should conform to the overall design of the book.

The design problems may be similar to those you first encountered on the table of contents page. If so, you could adapt — or duplicate entirely, if there are enough similarities — some of the ideas you had there.

Introduction

An introduction should do as its name implies — *introduce* the topic of the book. In some books it is a teaser, a brief summary telling the reader just enough to whet the appetite. It is also an opportunity to add up-to-date material that cannot be added to the main body of text at this late date.

Introductions are usually found only in books of nonfiction, and, more often than not, they appear as the last item of the front matter.

Prologue/Epilogue

These terms are rarely used today, except possibly in books of poetry or in play and movie scripts.

A *prologue* serves the same purpose as an introduction and can be part of the front matter.

An *epilogue* is a summary, or the concluding remarks, of a play or literary work, and, naturally enough, can appear at the back. Occasionally you will find an epilogue in modern books although the word can seem pretentious. I had an epilogue in my book about those two dogs in nineteenth-century San Francisco because

I felt that it was in keeping with that period. I would not have an epilogue in a manual such as this, however.

If you decide to use the words, you have the choice of spelling them with or without the final *ue* (*prolog, epilog*). Either way is acceptable, although the preference seems to be with rather than without, according to most American dictionaries. Again, use your chosen dictionary.

"Who reads it anyway?"

Before leaving the subject of front matter we should pause and consider the question "Who reads it anyway?"

William Safire, whose syndicated columns have given me a lot of pleasure and a great amount of sage advice, shocked me a few years ago by writing:

> Nobody reads prefaces. An introduction is considered part of a text, and is the piece of front matter closest to the first chapter; it usually gets skimmed, rarely perused. A preface comes before that, and is often a personal comment by the author apologizing for writing the work, or for being alive; in fact a couple of centuries ago, the preface was often called the *apology*. Even before the preface comes the most ignored part of what publishers call the *prelims:* the selling job on why the reader is obligated to read the rest of the book, usually by a famous name willing to shill for his buddy, the author, and it is called the foreword.

Safire went on to discuss a letter he had received from James A. Michener in which he (Michener) referred to forewords as "such puffery."

Since reading that particular column I have made my own inquiries with the result that, although I cannot agree "nobody" reads prefaces, I concede these two gentlemen are closer to the truth than I at first realized. In my (admittedly unscientific) study I concluded that two possible reasons for skipping the front matter text are that those pages are often too long or are usually printed in a smaller size type than is the main body of text.

Whereas most readers of scholarly works will peruse the entire text, no matter where in the book it is positioned and regardless of the size of type used, the average reader of the average book will skip lengthy introductory matter and will start right in at page 1 of the main text.

The lesson seems to be: If you insist on having this sort of preliminary matter keep it short, and give it an enticing layout, perhaps with an alluring headline. Or do as I have done: Put all that information into an introductory chapter and call it "Chapter 1."

14

Sections and chapters

The main body of text is divided into subdivisions, each of which has its own design considerations.

Half title (or, part title)

Separating the front matter from the main text is another half-title page (sometimes called *part-title page*). This is often a repeat of the bastard title page, with the name of the book positioned exactly as it was on that earlier page. If the book is a long one, and is divided into sections, this page could be a part-title page bearing the name and/or number of that section.

The reason for having a half-title page here is obvious: Your readers want to have a clear indication that the front matter is finished and that they are about to enter the main part of the book.

Throughout the book all part-titles should look alike and should be designed in such a way as not to be confused with the chapter titles.

Section titles . . .

The section title pages act as dividers for the various sections. They should stand out dramatically when you flip through the book. They can remain blank except for the title, or they can be given a special graphic treatment. In some books you will find these pages printed in a solid color, or black, with the type *reversed* out as white. Remember: This page should always be a recto.

. . . and their verso pages

To prevent a succession of blank verso pages you could put something on the back of the section title page to face the page on which the new text begins.

How about a photograph or illustration depicting the theme or topic discussed in that particular section?

If the book is a complex manual or textbook you could list here the contents of the section, either with or without page numbers.

Or you could print an appropriate epigram, positioning it carefully on the page so that it fits in with the basic design (aligned with, or in relation to, chapter titles, maybe; anywhere but in the dead center of the page).

You could place a *dingbat* (a piece of ornamental type) or an icon somewhere on the page — something appropriate either to the book in general or to the section in particular.

By electing to use one of these features you not only avoid too many blank pages but you establish a sense of continuity throughout your book.

Alternatively, you could use any one of these features on the section title recto page and start the text on the verso immediately following it.

Chapter openers

How's this terminology for openers?

- The page on which each chapter begins is called a *chapter opener.*
- The number of each chapter is called a *chapter head.*
- The title of each chapter is called a *chapter title.*

Whereas the title page establishes the theme of the book's design, the chapter openers are like flag bearers scattered throughout a parade, constantly reiterating that theme. Their design is another very crucial element in your book and should be treated with care and respect, but they should not compete with either the title page or the part-title pages.

Ideally the chapters should be of equal, or similar, length. If they are long and you have plenty of them, you should try to begin all of them on recto pages, even if it means leaving some facing pages blank. However, if the book is short and consists of only a few brief chapters, then these blank pages would become intrusive and wasteful. In such a case you would be better off starting the chapters wherever they fall, be it on verso or recto pages.

If the chapters do not have titles, and you need to conserve space, you could allow them to start on the same pages where the preceding chapters end. This is often done with novels, particularly when fast-moving action propels the reader onward. But even if you do it this way you need to consider the following points:

- The break should be clearly indicated with extra spacing between the end of one chapter and the line containing the new chapter's number.
- The chapter head (number) should be carefully placed between the two chapters, either flush left, flush right, or at any point in between, with slightly more space above than below to establish which chapter the head belongs to.
- If you cannot fit at least three lines of type at the bottom of a page following a new chapter head, do not start the chapter there.

Finding the formula. Your job now is to find a formula that can be applied to all chapter openers. Sketch several possibilities on pieces of paper which can be moved around under your master tracing guide until you find a combination that seems most appropriate.

The text on the first page of each chapter in most books starts about a third or half of the way down, with the number and/or title in the upper portion.

In a reference book the chapter head is used by the reader for quick identification and should be set in a type and position to make it most accessible.

In a novel without chapter titles the chapter head is the only means of identifying a new chapter.

In some books the chapter head is used merely as an element of graphic design and could be done away with entirely. Of course, you cannot do this if your text contains cross-references to specific chapters.

The word "chapter" is not always necessary and may actually be redundant in some cases. However, if the book is broken into sections AND into chapters you may need the word "chapter" to avoid confusion, unless you distinguish between the two by using roman

7
THE FASTEST BICYCLE
RIDER IN THE WORLD

THE FAME Major Taylor had won for his 1-mile world records in November 1898 was an asset his sponsor, Harry Sager intended to make good use of in publicizing his chainless bicycle. Sager decided to send the famous black rider around the country during the winter months to promote the much-discussed new departure in bicycle technology. Taylor would help the company establish dealerships, become in fact a traveling salesman, carrying with him for display the actual bicycle on which he had broken the records. Sager had high hopes for his invention in the coming year and great faith in Taylor.

In Waltham, Massachusetts, the Waltham Manufacturing Company gave away 1,000 photographs of racing cyclists and 1,000 handsome hat pins to the men and women who visited its store on Moody Street. There they advertised a GREAT EXHIBITION OF CYCLES AND PLENTY OF MUSIC, and promoted Taylor's presence. Their publicity proudly announced, "The famous rider arrived here yesterday and is demonstrating the merits of the Famous Sager Gear Orient Chainless. Friday and Saturday he will exhibit the Sager Gear to the ladies in the Ladies Department."

In Worcester, the chainless bicycle was exhibited at the Casey Brothers store on Main Street, and a large crowd showed up for the opening. The shop window was decorated with potted plants and flowers and the interior hung with the red and purple colors of the Orient Company. Taylor was, of course, the center of attraction, explaining the good points of the Sager gear with such skill and affability that it was clear the manufacturers had gotten themselves a topnotch salesman as well as a world-class rider.

In January 1899, on his way back to New York from the important Chicago Cycle Show, Taylor stopped off in Indianapolis for a few days to visit his family. There he exhibited the Sager bicycle at the shop of his old employer, Harry Hearsey, where, just a few years before, he

USA—CANADA, 1899

I

WHEN the Banon mail-coach calls at Vachères, it's always about noon.

You may well leave Manosque later, on the days when the usual passengers keep the coach waiting—when you reach Vachères, it's always noon.

It's as regular as clockwork.

It's even rather annoying to arrive there at the same time every day.

Michel, the coach-driver, once tried to stop at the crossroads of Revest-des-Brousses and spin a yarn with Fanette Chabassut, who keeps the Two Monkeys Inn, before setting out again at a leisurely pace. It made no difference. He just wanted to see; well, he did see!

9

Chapter openers for (left) *Major Taylor,* Bicycle Books, and (right) *Harvest,* North Point Press.

VI: Getting Power

To the edge of the earth
To the edge of the earth
To the edge of the earth
Snap all the people!
Snap all the people!
To the edge of the earth
To the edge of the earth.

Poisoning shaman's song,
Wintu

My Mountain

Trees, rocks, animals, mountain, springs, and other objects were not only alive, but they also had immense power. People sought that power by forming spiritual friendships and alliances with objects of great strength. An animal might approach a person in a dream and offer to share its power. Or a spring might approach. Or a ghost. Or a rock. Or even a mountain.

When I was still a young man, I saw Birch Mountain in a dream. It said to me: "You will always be well and strong. Nothing can hurt you and you will live to an old age." After this, Birch Mountain came and spoke to me whenever I was in trouble and told me that I would be all right. That is why nothing has happened to me and why I am so old now.

Not long after this, when I was bewitched, my power helped me out. I had been visiting one of the villages at Pitana Patu and had started back home to Tovowahamatu when I met a man who invited me to his house to have something to eat. It happened that a witch doctor lived in this vicinity, but thinking little of this, I ate a big meal of boiled meat and then went toward home. After walking a few miles, I became very ill and had a passage of blood. I went on, but became weaker and weaker, and when I reached the hot springs, a few miles north of Big Pine, I lay down under a bush. For a long time I lay there, and when it was nearly dark I got up and said to my soul, "Since my mountain has spoken and told me that I shall not die, why should I die here?" I went on to Tovowahamatu and made my camp just outside the village. The next day I entered the village.

A "stick doctor," who was my cousin and lived at Pitana Patu, was called. He arrived that night and came to my bed. He said: "How are you? Are you still there?" I was desperately sick by now and had hardly any strength to answer, "I am almost gone." Then

89

A section divider (left) and a chapter opener (right) for *The Way We Lived,* Heyday Books.

numerals for the sections and arabic figures for the chapters.

Keep titles uniform. If you are the author as well as the designer you can make sure that all the chapter titles are of equal length, thus saving yourself the problem of trying to give a uniform appearance to chapter openers when some titles are only a few words long and others occupy a couple of lines.

By starting the text low on the page you have a goodly amount of white space to display your title. Use it wisely! Move your rough sketch around under the tracing paper. See what happens to this white space when you center the title, and then when you place it flush left, or flush right. When you center it you break up the white space, and the overall effect becomes more crowded. If you position the title flush left, or flush right, the white space remains a more dramatic element.

Once you have decided where the title and number (if any) should be positioned on one chapter opener you must place all the others in the same position on their respective pages. It is a good idea to check these others before completing your layout, just to be sure the same style will work for all of them.

Sinkage. The distance between the top of the text area (not the top of the page) and the first line of your title is called *sinkage*. To maintain a healthy relationship throughout the book you should consider using the same sinkage not only for all the chapter openers but also for all the title pages, as well as for elements such as preface, introduction, bibliography, and index.

Remember to keep all the elements within your predetermined image area.

➤ *See Chapter 8 (**Display type**) for help on this.*

Paragraph indents

In most books, the first paragraph of any chapter, or section, is not indented, but starts flush left. This also applies to the paragraph immediately following a heading or subheading. Subsequent paragraphs are usually indented.

However, as explained on page 7:53, if your text lines are not justified you can forgo paragraph indentations and instead separate the paragraphs with extra line spaces. Either way, the idea is to break up solid blocks of text and make the page more inviting for your readers.

Display initials

The first letter of the first paragraph can become a design element if you choose to print it either as a *drop initial* or a *raised initial*. These are sometimes called *sunken initials* and *stick-up initials*. The generic term is *display initial*.

For many years these devices were considered an unnecessary expense, but they are making a comeback in book design. If used properly, they are welcome. If not, they can be the downfall of a design.

One reason for their revival is the mistaken belief that they can be inserted easily by a computer. In fact, with currently available software it is time-consuming to position a drop initial accurately, and many designers still resort to the traditional method of cutting and pasting it in position.

WHEN A DROP INITIAL IS USED it should align with the base of a text line and with the top of the letters that follow it. It is this alignment top and bottom that creates the problem for many computer users. As a result we now have what I call the *androgynous initial*, which is neither a true drop initial nor a true raised one. To gain the fullest effect you will need a fairly long paragraph so the initial will have something solid to drop into.

LET US SEE WHAT HAPPENS WHEN we begin with a two- or three-letter word — especially one that starts with an A or an L. The gap makes the word almost illegible. The lesson here is to try to avoid such short words at the beginning of a paragraph if a drop initial is to be used. Rewrite if necessary. Some designers extend the first line into the gap so that the second letter almost touches the drop cap.

WHEN YOU LOOK AT THESE two drop Ws one will appear correct while the other will look as if it has been indented slightly from the left edge of the text area. In reality, the first one extends slightly into the margin — thus making it look correct — while the one in this paragraph is flush left. The openness on the left side of the W creates the illusion that the letter is indented. To compensate, it should be extended slightly into the margin. Other capital letters that play a similar trick on the eye are: A, J, T, V, and Y. Be extra careful when using any of these. Looking at the line through half-closed eyes sometimes helps.

IF YOU USE A RAISED INITIAL, its base must align with the base of the first line of text. This paragraph need not be as long as one with a drop initial, although it would look better as a design element if it were. To get a better idea how this will work with your page layout, place your tracing paper over this page, and view each of these paragraphs separately while covering the other paragraphs with white paper.

Notice also that in each of these examples I have printed the rest of the word, plus a few words following it, in small capitals. This helps ease the transition from such a large letter back to the normal size of type and also provides a constant alignment for the top of a drop initial. It is not mandatory, but you should consider it.

The display initial can be of the same typeface used for the body text or the chapter title, or it can be of any other face — as long as it is compatible.

Once you decide to use either a drop or raised initial you should stay with that style throughout the book; do not use a drop initial here and a raised initial there.

Do not open some chapters with display initials and some without. It should be either all or none.

If you really want to be creative you could indent the first line of your opening paragraph AND use a raised initial. Then carry it one step further by indenting your chapter title and/or heading to align with the initial. However, this is the deep end of the pool and you should proceed with caution unless you are familiar enough with elements of design to carry it off effectively. The length of the title, the number of lines needed, and the typeface all play a vital part and must be considered very carefully.

Deleting running heads and folios

A running head does not appear on a chapter opener. Nor, in most books, does a page number, although this is more likely to be missed than is the running head.

Some publishers place a folio in the center of the bottom margin on chapter openers even when it appears at the top of all other pages. The reasoning seems to be that readers need a page number to know where they are. Purists would rather leave the folio off than disturb the book's design, noting that any intelligent reader can find the page without it, even when hunting a reference from the index.

Of course if the folios are placed on the bottom of ALL pages, then the question of what to do with them on chapter openers will not occur.

➤ *See Chapter 9 for more on folios.*

When you have decided on a basic design for your chapter openers, make a clean sketch of it on another sheet of paper, using exact proportions according to your tracing master guide, and you will have another page for your growing collection.

15

Back matter

The break between the main text and the back matter should be clearly defined. This is one area where you cannot avoid placing a section title on the right-hand page, even if you leave a blank page facing it. Page numbers continue in sequence, using arabic numerals.

Appendix

The purpose of the *appendix* is to present reports, tables, letters, or other items that are relevant to the book but would have been awkward to include in the main text, perhaps because of their bulk. Not all books have, or need, an appendix, but if there is one it should appear as the first item in the back matter.

If you have a lot of divergent information you can break it down into several appendices, titling them either numerically or alphabetically (Appendix 1, 2, 3; Appendix A, B, C).

The first appendix should start on a right-hand page. Subsequent appendices can start wherever they fall, either verso or recto.

The type can remain the same size as in the main body of text, although — particularly if space is a consideration — you can use a slightly smaller size.

As for *appendixes* vs. *appendices* — both are correct according to most American dictionaries, although *Chicago* uses only the former.

Notes

Footnotes rarely appear on the pages of text these days, except in some scholarly works. A few publishers place notes at the end of each chapter, but this can prove frustrating to the reader who wants to check out a foot-note while reading the text but cannot find the end of the chapter. The best place for such notes is a separate section at the back of the book, where they are more correctly referred to as *endnotes*.

If your notes use superscript numbers running con-secutively throughout the book, you can list them in numerical order in the back matter. You will help your reader if you break the notes down according to their chapters, using either the chapter titles or numbers as separate headings.

Here the question of type sizes comes up again. For variety, you could use a size smaller than that used for the main text, but not so small that it becomes difficult to read. The chapter titles and numbers can be either small capitals or boldface to aid the reader who needs to zero in on one particular footnote in a hurry.

Leave extra spacing between the different chapters.

➤   *See **Footnotes** in Chapter 9 for more on this topic.*

Glossary

A *glossary* is a dictionary of technical terms or special words. It is necessary in a book such as this one be-cause there are many words and phrases used in the publishing industry that are unfamiliar to most lay people.

If a book contains only a few words that the lay reader may not fully comprehend, it is often better to define them in parentheses within the body of text rather than create a separate glossary. But this becomes impracti-cal when such words are used only occasionally; the reader may have forgotten their meaning by the time they next appear.

As you can see, my method is to italicize and define the words on their first appearance. If there is a long break before they reappear, I either define them again or give clues to jog the reader's memory. I have also tried to give the most useful and precise definition of each word in the glossary at the back of the book.

The glossary should start on a right-hand page.

Words being defined should be printed flush left in either boldface or small capitals so they are easy to find. They can be followed by a period, a colon, a dash, or by no punctuation at all.

Some publishers capitalize all words being defined, while others capitalize them only if they are proper nouns. Whichever method you use, be consistent.

If the definition runs beyond one line you should indent the second and subsequent lines, leaving the first line flush left. This is called *hanging indentation*. I use this style for my glossary.

If all the definitions are less than one sentence long you do not need a period at the end of each definition. However, if some are and some are not, then all definitions should end with a period.

The words and their definitions must be listed in alphabetical order, with extra spacing between each item.

To help conserve space you can print the glossary in two columns, even if the rest of the pages have only one column. In larger format books you can set your glossary in three or four columns.

Some publishers combine the glossary with the index, printing the definitions in italics.

Other publishers place a brief glossary in the front matter, thus alerting readers to technical or unusual words they are about to encounter in the text.

Bibliography

A *bibliography* is a list of books (and sometimes magazine articles, newspaper articles, or scholarly papers) about a particular subject or person. *Chicago* devotes more than sixty pages to describing the many and varied ways a bibliography can be put together, but I will limit myself to a brief summary of the basic styles.

Perhaps the most commonly used style is the one that lists all references in alphabetical order according to the writer's name. In this case you will use the writer's last name followed by first name or initials, followed by title of book/article/paper, followed by the name of the publisher, then the year of publication. You may or may not want to include page and/or chapter numbers. The writer's name should be flush left, and all subsequent lines in the reference should indent slightly. The title of the book/article/paper should be italicized.

In addition to the information listed above, you should include the publisher's address (or at least the name of the city) so your reader can track it down. Also include the volume number, if applicable, and edition number. This practice will not only add credence to opinions you are expressing in your book but could induce other scholars to take the research another step forward. Who knows? They might even cite your book as one of their resources.

A bibliography may consist of any of the following lists:

- all of the books you used for your research ("Books Cited")
- only a few of your major sources ("A Selected Bibliography")
- all the books you can find on the topic ("Bibliography").

It is possible that in researching your topic you have gathered an impressive list of relevant books and documents that can be of great value to other scholars, and you should certainly create as complete a bibliography as you can.

Bibliographies play a major role in researching any topic. There are volumes of books devoted to bibliographic lists. Librarians always look for a bibliography (and/or an index) in a book. If you have one be sure to mention it in any publicity material you submit to libraries.

"Recommended Reading." On the other hand, the majority of readers do not even look at a bibliography. The very word can be intimidating. To make your list more enticing you could use a heading such as "For Further Reading," or "Recommended Reading."

If your book is of a scholarly nature you could print two lists — a bibliography AND a "Recommended Reading" list — thus appealing to both the serious scholar and the general reader.

Notice that I have broken my "Recommended Reading" list into groups relating to particular topics.

Usually books listed as "Recommended Reading" are still available in bookstores or libraries, or from the publishers. If you list rare and out-of-print books, or books that can be obtained only from far-away countries or esoteric sources, you should identify them as such.

Index

The index will probably be referred to more often than any other item in the back matter, which is why it must be placed in the most convenient position — at the very back, after all the other items.

You can have more than one index. One can list all the names and another all the topics, for example. Or you can have a combination of the two. No matter how many you have, they should help your readers find what they are looking for quickly and easily.

An entry consisting of one word followed by a long stream of page numbers can be very frustrating if readers have to check all those pages to find the pertinent information. When a particular word or phrase is mentioned several times in different contexts, the entries should be broken down into *main entries*, *sub-entries*, and *sub-sub-entries*. Professional indexers do not use more than five or six *locators* (page numbers or other reference markers) for a single entry.

Using a computer. It is common practice these days to create an index in word processing or desktop publishing programs. However, the result is usually nothing more than a list of words and locators without the subtle distinctions needed for entries, sub-entries, and the essential *See* and *See also* cross-references. A much better job can be done if you go through the computer printout and restructure it into a more functional index.

An index is a crucial part of any non-fiction book, particularly one that could be of use to other researchers. The better the index, the better the book. If you plan to do it yourself, you should study *Chicago*, which has 46 pages on the subject.

If you decide to seek professional help, contact:

> The American Society of Indexers
> 1700 18th Street N.W.
> Washington, D.C. 20009

and ask for a list of members in your vicinity.

Designing the pages of an index calls for extra care and attention because of the skimpy nature of the material. You'll make it easier for your reader if you divide the entries into alphabetical groups with large letters as signposts.

The type can be small, with a minimal amount of leading, and set in anything from one to four columns, as long as it is still readable.

Ideally, the index should start on a right-hand page.

Colophon

At one time the colophon appeared by itself on the last page, but now there is a tendency to place it on the copyright page. I discuss this topic fully in Chapter 12 and will not add more here other than a plea for the colophon's return to its traditional position at the end of the book.

16

Photographs and halftones

Before a black and white photograph can be printed in a book its subtle grays and blacks (called *continuous tone*) have to be converted to a mass of different-sized black dots (called *halftone*).

Because the printing press cannot vary the tones of ink it applies to paper, a subterfuge has to be employed to create the illusion of the different tones of gray seen in a photograph. The ruse works, and the human eye is tricked into believing it sees grays when in fact there is nothing but a variety of dots, all printed in the same tone of black.

The photograph is re-photographed through a halftone screen, the tiny holes of which create dots of different sizes depending on the amount of light projected from the original photograph. Brighter areas of the photograph will create lots of small dots surrounded by patches of the white paper surface. Darker areas of the photograph will create larger dots which huddle close together and have very little white space around them. The middle tones (grays) create medium-sized dots.

Once a photograph has been screened and printed in a book, magazine, or newspaper it should no longer be called a *photograph*. It is a *halftone*. In the printing trade photographs are often referred to as *continuous tones*, or *continuous-tone copy*.

© Walter Swarthout

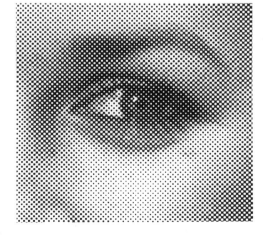

A question of dots

The screens used in the halftone process consist of crisscrossing lines. The more lines there are to an inch the more dots the screen will create. And the more dots a halftone has the sharper it will appear when printed.

Different paper surfaces demand different screens. A

coarse paper requires a coarse screen. Finer papers require finer screens.

Until a few years ago most newspaper halftones were made with 65 line screens, and the dots were clearly visible to the naked eye. As printing techniques and papers improved, newspapers started using finer screens — 80 lines, 100 lines, and 120 lines.

Most books are printed with 150-line halftones. If you are using coated papers you may want to consider 200-line screens, which will certainly give you a better quality image although the cost per halftone could be as much as $3 more. Discuss this with your printers.

You can go to a local photographer to get the halftone negatives made, or you can let your printers do the job for you. In the long run you're better off letting the printers do it since they know what will work best on their systems. Also — if the end result is not satisfactory — they will not be able to place the blame on whoever made the negative.

PMTs and Veloxes

Another way of reproducing photographs is to use an inexpensive screened print that has been made on photographic paper. One such print is called a *PMT* (Photomechanical Transfer), and another is called a *Velox*. The PMT is slightly cheaper than the Velox, and both are considerably cheaper than using the halftone negative method. However, because of their coarse screens, neither the PMT nor the Velox can produce the fine quality that is attainable with a halftone negative.

You can get PMTs and Veloxes made at a photocopy shop. They should be sized and cropped exactly as they will appear in the book because you will paste them on the actual pages you send to your printers.

➤ *See page 20:177.*

Where to put photos

One of your first design considerations when dealing with photographs will be where to place them in the book. Ideally they should appear close to their reference points in the text. If they cannot be on the same page they should be on either the page facing it or the one following it. However, it is sometimes necessary to bunch photographs together in one or more separate sections, without any apparent link to the text they are illustrating.

The determining factor will be your choice of paper. Although you can reproduce photographs on almost any paper these days, the fact remains that the better quality papers will give you better quality reproduction, for a higher price.

How essential are the pictures to your book? If they fill most of the pages, as in a photo essay, then you should consider printing the book entirely on a paper that has been coated with enamel.

If you have only a few photographs you can select any one of the standard smooth-surfaced papers that are available. These are less expensive than the coated papers and will allow you to print halftones on the same pages as the text.

But if you want to give your pictures an extra edge of quality without paying for the higher priced paper throughout the book, you can compromise by printing your text on a regular uncoated paper and then inserting one or more signatures of a coated paper on which to print the halftones.

If you do this you should seriously consider having your book Smyth sewn, or notch bound, rather than perfect bound because glue does not adhere well to enamel-coated paper.

➤ *See Chapter 23 for a discussion of different papers for different uses.*

Staying within the live area

In carefully designed books you will see that everything, except possibly the page number, appears within a clearly defined area on the page, leaving a uniform set of margins throughout the book. This area, as defined in Chapter 3, is known as the *live area* or the *image area*, as opposed to the *text area*, which contains only the text.

There are also books in which the entire double-page spread becomes a live area, with pictures *bleeding* off the page, and other elements spilling into what might normally be considered the margins. *Bleeds* require very careful planning if they are to be successful and economical, as I will explain later in this chapter.

You can also find books in which the designer establishes certain boundaries (i.e., margins) but fails to stay within them. In these books photographs or captions jut into the margins with an irregularity that disturbs the rhythm of the book's overall design, creating for the reader an uneasy feeling of something-is-wrong-but-I'm-not-sure-what.

To avoid pitfalls the novice publisher should decide at the outset to keep all elements — text, photographs, running heads, and captions — within a clearly defined image area. The only element that may appear beyond this area is the page number.

Built-in messages

Every picture has its own built-in design and message that must be taken into consideration if the page design is to function efficiently.

The issue is less critical if you have only one picture on each two-page spread. But the more pictures you add, the more they tend to vie with one another for attention. Rather than toss five or six pictures haphazardly on a spread you should first study them as a group to see how they interact. Place them side-by-side on the floor if necessary so you can stand back to see them in one glance.

Look at directional lines within each picture, and see how they flow (or contrast) with directional lines in the accompanying pictures.

The horizon line in one shot should align with the horizon line in an accompanying shot, thus creating a balanced reference point for the viewer.

Generally speaking, pictures of people should *face into the book*, although there are times when you can make a stronger statement by having them *face out*. Consider all the options and choose carefully rather than obstinately following the rules.

To avoid monotonous pages use halftones of different sizes and shapes, and try not to place all of them in the same position on the layouts.

A few suggestions

On the opposite page are a few basic layout ideas using grids already depicted in Chapter 4.

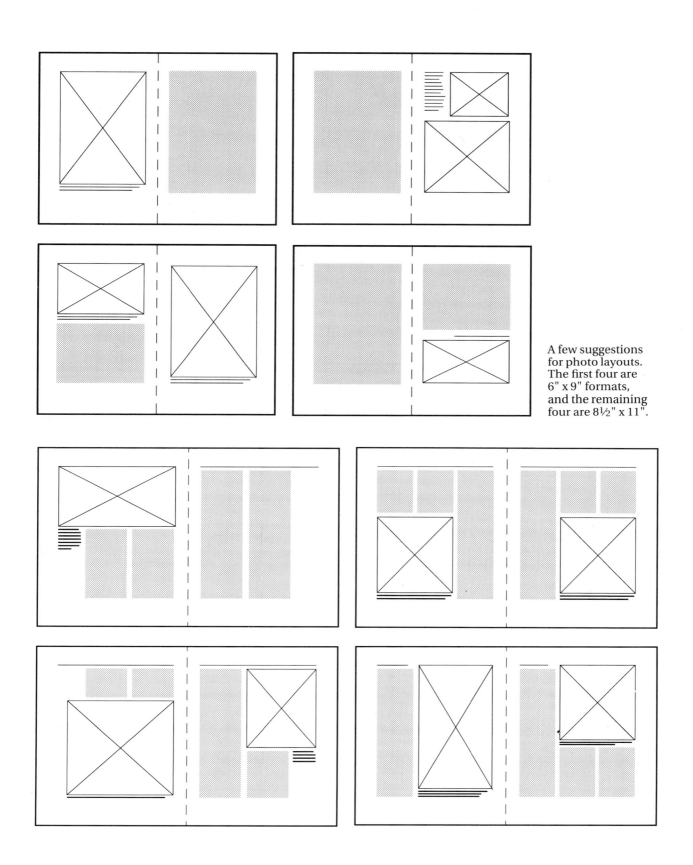

A few suggestions for photo layouts. The first four are 6" x 9" formats, and the remaining four are 8½" x 11".

Usually when a picture fills the image area you can eliminate the folio and running head to enhance the overall visual effect of the page. If a caption is needed it can go on the facing page or beneath the picture, in which case you would shorten the picture so that the caption does not extend outside the image area.

Cropping your photos

Unless they were carefully composed in the camera by the photographer most pictures can be improved by trimming extraneous areas. This is called *cropping*, and to do it efficiently you will need two "L" shapes cut from a piece of thick card stock.

Maneuver these L-shaped croppers across the photograph, blocking off areas that are not needed, until you have an image that presents its message without any distraction. When you decide how it is to appear on the page, place small marks in the white borders of the photograph. Do not mark the photographic image. If you don't want to mark the borders, you can lay tracing paper over the picture, trace the image very carefully, and then rule a box around the area you want retained.

As you crop, pay careful attention to vertical lines such as doorways, the sides of buildings, street lamps, etc. Make sure they are squared off.

Printers need an extra $\frac{1}{16}$" on each side of the image when preparing the plates for printing. If a picture does not have a white border, $\frac{1}{16}$" will be trimmed off all sides of the actual image. This is one good reason why you should never cut a photograph to conform with your crop requirements.

You can buy croppers from a photography store, or you can make your own. The best ones are those cut from card stock that is black on one side and white on the other: The black side is best when cropping a light photograph, and vice versa. If the largest photograph you have is 8" x 10", then make the inside measurements of the L-shapes no smaller than 8" x 10".

How to scale your pictures

You have selected the pictures you want in the book. You have decided where on the pages they will appear. And you have a rough idea of what sizes you want them to be. Now you have to figure out how each picture is

© Walter Swarthout

By cropping extraneous areas of a photo you can get a more dramatic effect and make better use of the same amount of space on the page, as illustrated (left). An even tighter crop can be seen below. A ½-point rule is printed flush around three of these images to HOLD IN the light edges; otherwise the image tends to float, as can be seen lower right. All are from the same photo, which is of Bolshoi Ballet Master Shamil Yagudin instructing students at the Marin Ballet Center for Dance.

going to fit in the space you have allotted for it. This you do by *scaling*.

You can scale the cropped image so that it fits in a particular shape and size on the page, or you can scale an area on the page so that it will accommodate the image. Either way the principle is the same: All dimensions of each image will reduce or enlarge at the same proportion.

When you reduce the short side of an 8" x l0" photograph to 4" (50%) the long side automatically reduces to 5" (also 50%), giving you a final image of 4" x 5". The image is said to be *reduced 50%*. Similarly, if you enlarge the short side of 5" x 7" by 50% you will end up with an image that is 7½" x 10½".

One way to scale an image is to use a circular proportional slide rule which you can buy at any art supply store. Another is to figure it out mathematically, determining the percentage of reduction or enlargement needed in order to fit one size into the other.

A third method is to draw a diagonal line through the known dimensions and create a rectangle representing the new dimensions. At first this may seem complicated but, with practice, it becomes quite simple.

Reducing to fit. Let us assume you want to reduce a photograph to fit a particular space on the page. First you place tracing paper over the photo and lightly draw a box around the cropped area. Separate the tracing paper from the photo and then draw a diagonal line from the lower left corner of the box. Mark on the bottom line of the box you have drawn the width you want the finished image to be, and then draw a vertical line beyond the point where it hits the diagonal. Extend to the left a horizontal line from the meeting point of vertical and diagonal lines. This smaller box represents the size your photograph will be on the page.

Unless you have done this many times before, chances are your final dimensions will not agree with those you drew on your layout, and you may have to adjust your layout to these actual figures.

Usually one of the dimensions, vertical or horizontal, will be less flexible than the other, depending on the image, or on your own needs. You can afford to vary slightly in one direction, but not in the other. Use the most critical dimension in starting the scaling process.

© *Walter Swarthout*

I sometimes take a short-cut by determining only the most critical dimension and then making an educated guess at the other, waiting until after I have finished scaling to see what I get.

Enlarging the image. The process is similar if you need to enlarge a photograph. First trace the cropped area, and extend the left-hand vertical and base lines a few inches. Then draw your diagonal from the lower left corner beyond the upper right corner. Mark the most critical of your dimensions on either the left vertical or on the baseline, and complete the new box as you did when reducing.

A photographic image deteriorates as it is enlarged but improves as it is reduced. Remember this if you are enlarging images. If you have the negatives, you would be better off making larger prints than trying to enlarge from small prints.

Same-size heads. A point to keep in mind if you are scaling two or more portraits for the same page is that — unless for some reason you intend to stress the importance of one over another — the heads of all people should be proportionately the same. This is one of those taken-for-granted rules you do not often find in design books, but it is considered very important.

Evaluating your photos

If the print you start out with is not of good quality you cannot expect it to reproduce well.

A major consideration is the contrast between black and white. In other words, the blacks and whites in the image should be clearly defined, and there should be a good range of grays in between. Otherwise the print is *flat* and will appear muddy on the page of your book. Another consideration is sharpness. Check to see if the critical areas are in focus.

Make sure there are no stains, creases, or tears on the print. If you must use a damaged print take it first to a professional retoucher who can *retouch* (repair, or alter) it for you. Look in your telephone directory under "Photo retouchers," or inquire at a photography store.

There are occasions when a flat and out of focus photo has enough significance to warrant using it. At a time like this consider printing it small, but in a strategic position. Printing it large only accentuates its faults.

Captions

First we should clarify our terms. A *caption* is defined variously as the heading above a picture and as the descriptive passage under it. *Webster's Ninth New Collegiate Dictionary* lists both definitions for the same word. *Chicago* states specifically that a *caption* is "a title or headline, especially one placed in the traditional location, above the illustration," and it calls the descriptive passage beneath the illustration a *legend*.

In this book I use the word *caption* to mean the descriptive passage rather than the title or headline, since in my experience most people use it this way.

Captions can appear on the left, right or top of the image, as well as beneath it. When several pictures appear on a page all captions can be grouped together, as long as they are written so as to link them to their respective images. There are occasions, of course, when a caption is not necessary. Just be consistent and use the same method throughout the book.

Choice of typeface is important because captions should not be confused with the regular body text. If they are not too lengthy they can be printed in italics. You can use a smaller size of the text typeface so long as it is not placed in such a way as to be read as part of the text. This is sometimes the problem when halftones and their captions are the same width as a column of text.

Some purists will set the lines of long captions exactly the same width as the halftone, adding extra words if necessary to ensure the last line is complete, thus creating a neat box-like effect to emphasize the shape of the halftone. This is all right if the book's text is justified, but it may look odd if used with ragged-right text.

Credit lines

Photographers are particularly sensitive about having their names and copyright notices appear as close to their image as possible because without it their legal rights are weakened. Ideally, it shoud be

© 1990 John Doe
or
Photo: © 1990 John Doe

either beneath the halftone or running vertically along the right-hand side of it.

Some photographers will not insist on using the © symbol and will be happy with just their names, no matter how small the type, as long as it is legible. Unless you have a very specific house style you can use whatever wording the photographer requests.

You may elect to list all photo credits in one place, either in the front matter or in the back matter, if you are dealing with several different photographers.

The same guidelines apply if you borrow photographs or prints from institutions or individuals, although here you would print something to the effect of

> Photo courtesy The Bancroft Library

alongside or beneath the halftone.

Bleeds

When a picture runs off the edge of a page it is called a *bleed*. It can bleed off one edge only, or two, or three, or all four. When it bleeds off all four edges it is called a *full bleed*.

Bleeds are created by printing pages larger than the final trim size and then cutting away the excess. If your book is smaller than one of the standard sizes (if, for example, it is 5" x 8" or 8" x 10") then there should not be a problem, since the pages will not occupy the entire sheet anyway. You run into difficulties when you use a standard size such as 6" x 9" or 8½" x 11" because they take up the entire sheet except for a narrow unprintable margin where the press's gripper grabs hold of it.

If you have only a few pages with bleeds your printer can adjust the sheets on the press to prevent the bleeds from falling in that unprintable margin. Some printers will do this without charge, but if your design calls for too many bleeds, creating a lot of extra work for the press people, you will have to pay for it. Your printer may decide that the only way to do the job is by using larger sheets of paper, adding greatly to your production costs.

If you want to use bleeds, talk it over with your printer as early as possible and decide whether the additional costs are worthwhile.

When cropping a bleed photograph you must give the printer an extra ¹⁄₁₆" so it can be trimmed.

Duotones

Duotones are halftones printed in two colors, usually black and brown, black and gray, or black and blue. The process can be expensive since it requires more plates, more negatives, and extra presswork, but the final effect can be well worth the expense if you have the right images. Discuss it with your printers.

Unobtrusive type

In photo essay books, when the pictures are more important than the words, a light and unobtrusive typeface is sometimes more appropriate. Select one with thin strokes and a tall x-height. An elegant touch can be added by printing all the text (assuming there is not too much of it) in gray ink rather than black ink. This helps subdue the text while accentuating the photographic images. Seek guidance from your printers on this point because there are many shades of gray ink. You don't want it to be too light or too dark.

Summing up

- Be selective. Don't use a picture just because you have it. A few good, strong images are better than a lot of mediocre ones.
- Let each photograph determine its own shape, size, and position. Be guided by its built-in design and message.
- If necessary, crop your photographs to delete confusing and unnecessary detail, and to strengthen the overall image.
- Generally when you have two or more portraits on a spread, the heads of the people should be proportionately the same.
- Good, powerful images should be printed large.
- Pictures which have something to say, but are less powerful as images, can often express their message better if printed small but placed strategically on the page.

17

The cover design

A cover should reflect the theme of a book in a manner compatible with the book's interior design.

Where and how you intend to sell your book will influence how you design its cover. If you want to sell it in stores the cover has to be enticing enough to catch the eye of the browser. It has to be a mini-poster, bright and colorful, and easily read from a distance. It has to stand out from the masses that surround it.

If your main thrust will be through direct mail you won't need to advertise on the cover because the job of enticing a buyer will rest with the flier or brochure. However, since most likely the cover will be reprinted in black and white and reduced dramatically for the brochure, you have to take extra care with the design. It should not be too dark, nor too cluttered, and there should be sufficient contrast in the colors so they are discernible when reproduced without color.

Study the competition
Now is the time for another field trip to bookstores, this time to study the competition and to see what the current fashion is in cover designs. Be critical. If you see a cover you don't like, don't just exclaim and put it down with an I-can-do-better-than-that sigh. Examine it closely and see WHY you don't like it. Sometimes we learn more from bad examples than from good ones.

When a book attracts your attention, study it closely to see what caused it to stand out from the others.

Most major publishing houses have one person designing the interior of a book and another doing the cover. This is because not all professional artists like to, or can, design both. Unfortunately this sometimes results in covers that are totally unrelated to what is inside, either in theme or design, much to the annoyance of readers, who feel deceived. This can be avoided by not bringing in the cover artist until the rest of the book is designed, or at least until the general concept has been established. He or she is then given a copy of the manuscript, or an early set of proofs, along with details of the basic interior design, and is told to come up with something appropriate and compatible.

Using an artist

You may prefer to have an artist do the cover once you have established the basic interior design.

Tell the artist to give you a few rough sketches to look at before getting too involved. Study these carefully, visualizing how they will look when complete. If you cannot make up your mind between a couple of ideas ask for these specific ones to be done again, with more detail. But be fair to your artist and do not apply too many restrictions, or you may end up with something that could have been better if you had not stifled his or her creative energies.

Color is crucial to design. Since colors are available today in such a vast array you should SEE what your artist has in mind rather than be told this part is red, that part is green, and there it is mauve. Most professional cover designers will give you a full-color rendering of the design using close approximations in paints, inks, or overlays, or at least by attaching PMS color swatches. These swatches are part of the Pantone Matching System — a standard set of colors used in the graphic arts and printing industries and generally referred to by numbers, as in *PMS 151* (a particular shade of orange).

Four colors for the price of two

With careful manipulation of these colors and overlays it is possible to get three colors, and sometimes more, when paying for only two. Black type on a white background is considered *one-color printing*. If you add a color to the background (blue, for example), you have black on blue, or *two-color printing*. If you *reverse out* a line of type or section of the illustration by letting it appear as white (the color of the paper), then you have three colors — black, blue and white — and are still paying for only two. But if you use yellow ink instead of black for your type, you can get a bonus color (green) by overlapping it with the blue in specific areas. You will then have yellow, green, blue and white while using a two-color process.

The dust jacket of *The Chicago Manual of Style* is an excellent example of impressive two-color printing: orange background, white (reversed out) title, and black ink for all other text.

There is a knack to doing this effectively, and if you want to try it you should first discuss your ideas in detail with the printers. Be prepared for some additional costs for each of these separate steps.

This multicolor process should not be confused with the 4-color process used for printing photographs. In that process only the three primary colors (yellow, cyan, and magenta) are used, in conjunction with black.

Doing it yourself

If you are doing the cover yourself, work with rough sketches until you have the final concept clear in your mind. Then move on to the full-size piece of paper.

Read again the chapter dealing with display type (Chapter 8), paying particular attention to the comments about the different effects you can achieve according to where on the page you place the title.

It may help, also, to read again page 11:94 where I refer to the common thread that should link the cover with the title page.

The only two elements that consistently appear on covers are the title and the author's name. Word-only covers can be very impressive if you use the right typeface and colors, especially if you position them creatively.

Black and white in color

Photographs do not have to be printed in full color. You can use black and white photos and print them on a light-color background. Or you can print them as *duotones.* A duotone is made by printing two negatives in different colors — usually black plus one other such as brown or blue. The process requires skillful work by the printer to keep both negatives in register, and the result can be quite dramatic. You get a more complete range of tones than with one-color printing.

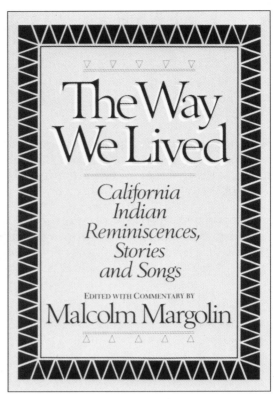

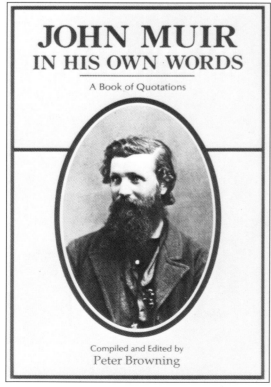

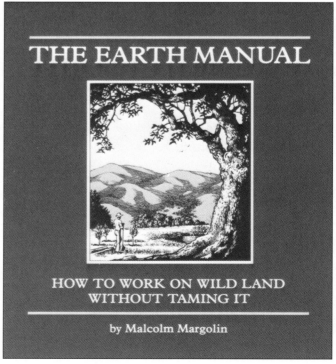

If you want a 4-color photograph on the cover be pre-pared to add $500–$1,000 to your production costs. Four separate negatives are made — yellow, magenta (red), cyan (blue), and black — and these are printed one at a time on the press. The four colors combine to create all the colors you see in the final image. This process, which is called *color separation*, is now being challenged by *scanners* — computers that do the job faster and cheaper.

You can keep your costs down by not having type or any other element touch or overlap the photograph. If any element is to overlap, it must first be placed on a separate sheet of film and then placed in register with the other color negatives. This is not a problem if the overlapping element prints as black, but if you want it in a different color then the process becomes more complicated, and the price escalates accordingly.

Using stock photos

Appendix C lists a number of stock photo resources that supply pictures to publishers and advertising com-panies. You can contact one or more of these if you need a photograph and you don't have one that is suitable.

Included in the appendix are a few government agen-cies that will let you have copies of famous old photo-graphs and paintings for only the cost of production and mailing. This historic shot of moon-walking astro-naut Buzz Aldrin is one of thousands of U.S. govern-ment photos that are available to the public and not subject to copyright. All you have to do is write and ask.

When dealing with any of the commercial sources you must read the fine print of their contracts very care-fully. In most cases you will have to print a credit line indicating the name of the photographer and the source. Permission may be granted only for *one-time use*, limited specifically to use either on the cover OR inside the book. Where and how you place the picture may determine how much you'll have to pay.

If you use the picture on the cover of your book, and then use a photo of the cover in your promotional material, technically you are getting a second use from the shot. Most agencies will not charge extra for this, but it is better to clarify the point up front than to have a legal battle (or a bill for extra usage) later on. Send a request, in writing, stating you intend to use the cover

PHOTO: NASA
Astronaut Buzz Aldrin walking on the moon, July 1969.

as part of your promotional material. If you want to use the picture again in your brochure as a separate image, not as part of the cover, you should also make this clear. And be sure you get written permission.

The easiest way is to send two copies of a letter explaining what you want to do with the picture and include at the bottom something to the effect of "Permission granted by: —— (signature), —— (title)." Ask for one copy to be signed by someone of authority and returned to you in the stamped envelope you enclose.

The spine

There is more to a cover than the front. You still have to design the back cover, and the spine.

The thickness of the spine depends on the thickness of the book, which is determined by the thickness of the paper. To avoid errors, ask your printers to work this out for you.

With the jacket of a hardcover book you should also allow for the thickness of the front and back boards.

The three elements usually found on a spine are the author's name (sometimes with room only for the last name), the book's title, and the publisher's logo or name.

The ideal spine is one that is thick enough to let you print these words horizontally so you don't have to crane your neck reading the title when the book is upright on a shelf. You may have to hyphenate a word or two, but that is better than squeazing in the words and using type too small to be read.

Failing that, the words should be printed from the top to the bottom of the book, so they appear upright when the book is lying face-up on a table.

Use the same typeface as on the cover, in a color that will be easy to read. If part of the front cover illustration bleeds across the spine it should not interfere with the legibility of the lettering.

Do not let the type get too close to the edge of the spine; leave at least $\frac{1}{16}$" all around on a paperback spine and at least $\frac{1}{8}$" on a hardcover spine.

Remember that when the book is sitting on a shelf,

either in a store or in a home, all that can be seen is this thin strip, usually less than an inch wide. Make sure that it stands out from other books.

The back cover

Most people pick up a book and immediately turn to the back cover looking for the *blurb* — the pitch explaining what the book is about and why the browser should become a buyer.

It is as if the browser says to you, the publisher: "Okay. I've picked up your book. Now tell me what it's all about." Your job is to whet the appetite, enticing that person to flip through the pages, then go directly to the cash register. If you fail this test, the book is returned to the shelf and forgotten.

While the book is in its final stages you can send out proofs and ask people to write testimonials. These always look impressive on the back cover, especially if the names are well known.

Or you can write a brief summary of what the book is about, highlighting specific areas of interest.

In the case of a self-help book or a manual it is a good idea to print an abbreviated version of the table of contents, or a list of topics expounded upon in the book.

You could also include a brief paragraph about the author, and possibly a photograph.

The back of a paperback should be treated with the same respect and seriousness as the front, and you'll be wasting a good selling tool if you leave it blank. It is different with a hardcover because most browsers look on the flaps of a jacket for the blurb. Usually a summary of the book's topic appears on the front flap, and a biographical note and photograph of the author appear on the back flap.

The bar code

There are certain elements that are mandatory if you are selling your book in stores: The ISBN, the price and/or the Bookland EAN bar code symbol — that block of lines we see on everything from refrigerator packing cases to milk cartons, and from comic books to candy bars. I say "and/or" because the symbol includes both the ISBN and the price.

Until recently, bookstores were satisfied if you printed the ISBN in the lower right corner of the back cover, and the price in the lower left. Now they say you must use the bar code instead, placing it where the ISBN used to go. Designers have tried to resist but are losing the battle. The policy of many stores is: "No code, no sale."

For about $20 you can have a code and symbol created for your book by writing to one of several manufacturers and giving them the appropriate information. Within a few days you will receive a piece of film which you then apply to the artwork of your cover.

Ask R.R. Bowker for a list of bar code manufacturers when you apply for your ISBN.

➤   *See ISBN, Chapter 12.*

A "country" called Bookland. Different symbols are used for different applications. The one used on trade books is called Bookland EAN because the first three digits (978) represent the "country" Bookland — a code that is used throughout the world to identify books. EAN stands for European Article Number, even though the system is now used beyond the boundaries of Europe.

Mass market books which are sold in supermarkets and other merchandise stores use the UPC (Universal Product Code), which is similar to the one used on cereal boxes and wine bottles.

The symbol illustrated here is the one imprinted on the back of the book you are reading. Following the Bookland code (978) are the first nine digits of the book's ISBN. The final digit of the series acts as a verification for this particular numerical combination.

Adjoining that block is the *add-on* which represents the price of the book. The first digit (5) identifies the currency as U.S. dollars. The remaining four are the price, without the decimal point ($24.95). If a price is less than $10.00 a leading zero is added, as in 50695 ($6.95).

On some books you will see 90000 where normally the price appears. This usually indicates that the book is sold in more than one country, in which case the sales clerk must look at an international price list printed elsewhere on the back cover. It could also mean the publisher was anticipating a price increase.

Bookstores claim they save time and money when this code is scanned by a pen-like device. Not only will it ring up the price on the cash register, but it will adjust the inventory and also facilitate ordering more books or returning unsold copies to the publishers.

This is how the system works, according to *Machine-Readable Coding for the U.S. Book Industry*, a booklet issued by the Book Industry Study Group, Inc.:

> The ability of the scanners to decode a symbol is based on measuring the bar and space widths and determining their arrangement. As the scanner moves across the symbol, it recognizes the bar/space edges by the changes in their reflectivity. These changes in reflectivity, and their relationship, are called the Print Contrast Signal (PCS). Different color densities, ink quality and types of substrates will all affect the resultant PCS. The "dark" bars are manifest by a low reflectivity; the "light" spaces by a high reflectivity.

According to this same source, the bars must always be the darker color, although not necessarily black. They can be dark blue; reflex blue, process blue, and cyan are suggested.

Also, the spaces do not have to be white. They can be yellow or red, as long as there is no blue or black in the background. In other words, even if you have a solid color covering the back you don't have to introduce the jarring effect of placing a patch of white there. By being more selective with your background color the bar code need not overpower your design. This is because the scanner reads dark blues as black, and it reads reds and yellows as white.

Cover protection

You need to give careful consideration to the SURFACE of the cover. It is no use spending all that money and time designing a beautiful cover if the ink later wears off, or if the cover cracks, curls, or tears easily.

The most popular choice of paper for a dust jacket, or for the cover of a paperback, is one that is .010" thick and coated lightly on one side. This is refered to as 10pt C1S. A slightly thicker sheet — 12pt C1S — is also available.

This coating creates an excellent surface to print on because it prevents the ink from sinking into the paper.

Instead, the ink sits on the top of this smooth surface and looks sharper and more precise than if used on an uncoated surface. The disadvantage is that, when the surface is rubbed against another book, or is handled roughly, the ink begins to *scuff* (wear off), leaving white blotches of paper showing through. This is particularly true of books that have a large area of ink on the cover — as, for example, books with a color background printed over the whole surface.

There are a number of ways to combat this, although each has its own disadvantage.

Varnish, and shrink wrap. Some printers apply a varnish to hold the ink on the paper, and then suggest you pay to have the books *shrink wrapped.* In other words, the books will be sealed tightly in a clear plastic wrap, either individually or in groups of four or five, for shipment to you.

DISADVANTAGE: The varnish offers very limited protection to the ink and, once the plastic wrap is removed, the covers are in danger of being scuffed while rubbing against other books on a tightly packed shelf. Although varnish is the cheapest form of protection, by the time you have paid for shrink wrapping you are no longer saving money.

UV coating. You can have a liquid ultraviolet coating applied to the cover to protect the ink. This method is superior in some respects to varnish or lamination since it gives you a choice of either a dull or a glossy finish, and its surface has a pleasant texture. In price, it falls somewhere between the varnish and the lamination process.

DISADVANTAGE: The coating has a tendency to crack when bent, as at the edge of the spine, and at the folded edge of the dust jacket's flaps.

Film lamination. Perhaps the most popular method today is *film lamination*, in which a thin, clear sheet of film is applied to the cover. This adds a high gloss, as well as making the cover almost impossible to tear. Its hard, smooth surface resists coffee stains and finger marks. It will add approximately 5 cents to the cost of a cover and 10 cents to the cost of a dust jacket.

DISADVANTAGE: In damp weather the film sometimes curls the cover of paperbacks. This seems to be less of a problem today, although it is still one to be contended with. Laminated dust jackets are not affected in quite the same way since they are held down when the flaps are tucked under the cover boards.

Antique finish paper. Another choice you have for the cover or jacket is an antique finish paper which, because it has not been coated, is more like a blotter. It will soak up the ink well, does not need to be varnished or laminated, and will not scuff. It should work out to about the same price as using a C1S sheet with varnish. Most printers carry these sheets in various weights, usually 50-lb, 65-lb, and 80-lb. The most popular is the 65-lb. These papers come in different colors, as well as in white. They are more expensive than regular papers, although you will save money by not having to add a color background if you use a colored sheet, and you will not be adding lamination or varnish.

DISADVANTAGE: The surface is rough, and lacks the sheen we expect to find on the cover of a book. But there are books that could turn this to an advantage, which is why I include it here — another opportunity for you to think creatively.

II

PRODUCTION

18

Finding professional help

When it comes to the production of your book you have a number of alternatives.

- Have someone set the type and provide you with galleys, which you will then cut and paste onto boards for shipment to the printing company.
- Have the typesetter prepare and paste up the boards (or reproduction proofs, if your printers prefer it that way).
- Do the whole thing yourself on a computer, using a desktop publishing program.
- Hand your manuscript over to a book production service and let them do everything for you — typesetting, design, layout, etc.

Obviously the cost will vary with each of these alternatives. To pay a book production service to do everything will cost more than if you only have someone else set the type while you do the rest. But for many people this is still preferable because the book will be in more experienced hands throughout the entire process.

But even if you decide to use a service, you should be familiar with what they are doing. This chapter is for you as well as for the publisher who prefers to take on more of these tasks.

How to find the right people
In your local library you will find a copy of *Literary Market Place* (popularly referred to as *LMP*) — an invaluable book listing all the resources a publisher needs, from a typist who can prepare your manuscript to people who can review your published book and salespeople who can distribute it. This should be the first place to look.

If you live in one of the major metropolitan areas your local telephone directory will provide you with several names to choose from. Obviously the closer you are to all of these services the easier it will be for you.

The book production service

Book producers can relieve you of all — or some — of the labors of publishing. They can begin with your original manuscript and go all the way to shipping the finished product to bookstores. If you want them to, they will even go as far as sending copies to reviewers, and taking care of marketing and publicity.

The book will still be YOURS. Throughout the process you remain in control, making all the decisions concerning design, production, and promotion — based on the guidance they offer you. And you pay only for the services they provide.

You will find names and addresses in the LMP. Write to a few of them and ask about their specific services. Find out their prices, and ask to see samples of their work. Give them an idea of what you need, and ask how much time they will require to do it.

In addition to studying the samples they supply, check the quality of their promotional material. A company that sends out a shoddy self-promotional piece cannot be relied upon to provide quality work for its clients.

Not the same as subsidy presses. Do not confuse book production services with s*ubsidy presses* (or, *vanity presses*), which offer similar services but under very different conditions, and at a greater cost to you. When you deal with a subsidy press you will have to pay all production costs PLUS a percentage on every copy of the book sold. You will have little, if any, control on the book's design, or on such vital aspects as choice of typeface, paper, or even the number of copies being printed.

Furthermore, if the promised sales do not materialize, you will have to buy back copies for yourself!

The typesetter

There should be no shortage of typesetters in your area. The tricky part is finding one who does more than business cards, fliers, newspaper advertisements, and handouts for new pizza parlors. What you want is someone who has worked on books — someone who can help you select the right typeface for your particular manuscript, who is familiar with the nuances of page layouts, and who has time to devote to hundreds of pages of typesetting.

Visit more than one typesetter, checking out not only their prices but also the variety of typefaces they have available. In doing so, notice how they respond to your questions. Do you get the impression that they will guide you through this unfamiliar territory? Do they take the time to explain things to you? Do you feel that they are talking down to you?

Ask to see samples of other books they have done. Look at these carefully, paying attention to the quality of the type and the way it is set.

As explained in Chapter 7, most typesetters can offer a type style book indicating the different typefaces they have. If you want a face they do not have, will they get it for you? Some will charge extra for this, others won't.

The word processing and page layout programs used by computerized typesetters are constantly being upgraded, and some of the small shops cannot afford to keep up with the latest technology.

If your book consists mainly of basic text almost any professional typesetter can do the job for you. But if you need features like equations, complicated tables, unusual fractions, or complex graphics, you must be very selective when looking for a typesetter. By making your demands known early you can avoid the frustration of discovering halfway through the project that you are working with the wrong typesetter — one who cannot give you what you want.

Printing companies

LMP can also help you locate a printing company. You should wait until most of the typesetting and layout is complete before you begin these overtures, because by then you will have a better idea of how many pages your book will need. Also, when printers send you their quotes they stipulate that the figures will be applicable only for a certain period (usually 30 or 60 days) because of the fluctuating prices of paper and labor.

However, if your book requires enamel coated paper, or some other special stock, you should begin these overtures early enough for the printers to order and receive the paper.

Appendix A lists several short-run printers who work with small publishers.

The artist

If you want a professional artist to design the cover or draw some illustrations for inside the book, look for names, addresses, and phone numbers in *LMP* or in your local telephone directory. Do not be shy about interviewing these people and asking to see their portfolios; that is the best way for you to find out who is most suited to your assignment, and often it is the only way for them to get clients.

Artists, being creative people, can be temperamental. You as a writer may also be temperamental. The work you will be creating together will be crucial to the success of your book, so it is imperative that you find someone with whom you can work amicably, without fear of clashing egos. Pay attention to any vibrations, good or bad, which you may sense during the interview.

The editor

Someone once said, "Every writer needs an editor." I don't know who that someone was, but the statement is true enough — especially if the writer is also the publisher, and if there is nobody between the typist and the typesetter to spot inconsistencies of style, or to point out that what is written is not what the writer had in mind.

If your book had been accepted by one of the major publishing houses it would automatically be handed over to an editor. So why not call upon the services of an editor now?

There are *copy editors,* who can go through the manuscript with an eye on such basics as spelling, punctuation, and grammar, and then there are *developmental editors,* who can help with the deeper aspects of a manuscript, such as clarity and cohesiveness.

Instead of viewing editors as dreaded English teachers, or people out to change your style to their style, you should look upon them as an audience, rather like an actor's audience at a dress rehearsal. The way they respond will be a clue as to how your readers will respond. If an editor cannot understand what you are saying, then it is likely your readers will not understand either.

It is not sufficient to hand your manuscript to friends or relatives. Unless they are professional editors they might be so excited about your having written a book that is going to be published that they are unable to be objective and give a true evaluation. Better to pay a professional to do the job for you — someone who can approach the task without any preconceived ideas or emotions.

A delicate relationship. There is probably no more delicate relationship between any two people in the entire publishing industry than that between an author and an editor. Many authors are incensed at the thought of anyone tampering with their words, and they believe that only harm can come from allowing an editor near their work.

In the opinion of one author I know, only one-third of what an editor suggests is beneficial, while one-third is harmful, and one-third is of no benefit or harm. "Which means," my friend concludes, "that two-thirds of what the editor does is useless or worse and creates great aggravation and expenditure of time and effort by the author."

To which one can add: "That depends on the editor and on the author."

The editor's decision is not sacrosanct, and the author should have the final say in any disagreement since it is the author's name that appears on the book's cover. But when the talents of a good editor are combined with the talents of a good author, the outcome should be a well-written book.

Different editors charge different rates. Some work by the hour, some by the page, while others charge a flat rate for the whole job. Speak to several editors until you find the right one. Some will offer to do a *sample edit*, which means they will edit four or five pages without charge just so you can see how they respond to your work.

Look for editors in *LMP*, or in your telephone directory. Better still, speak to other publishers (large or small) to find out whom they use.

Paying for these services

To produce a professional-looking book a publisher should act like a professional and should be prepared to seek — and pay for — the services of people who are professionals in their own fields. Rather than go without such services for lack of funds, you could approach local schools or colleges to find students who are studying these skills. Also, you may find someone who is just starting out in the business and who would be happy to work for less than standard rates just to gain the experience — and for the chance of an acknowledgment in your book.

With each one of these people — typesetter, printer, artist, editor — as well as anyone else you may call on for help, you must be as precise as possible when giving instructions. Misunderstandings cause bad feelings and waste time and money, and they can be avoided if you put instructions in writing, even if just in an informal letter, with copies for both of you. These people need to know exactly what is expected of them, and you need to know how much you will be paying for their services.

19

Dealing with typesetters

You can keep costs to a minimum by making sure the work you give the typesetter is clean, easy to read, and as free of errors as you can make it. In addition to the usual criteria (8½" x 11" white paper, double-spaced, etc.), you should consider the following:

- Are your instructions concerning type sizes for main text, extracts, footnotes, captions, etc., clearly indicated? (Chapter 9)
- Does the typesetter know the exact width and depth of the text area on each page? (Chapter 3)
- Are you specifying a maximum number of consecutive lines with word-breaks? (page 9:76)
- If your type is not being set justified, do you want a minimum line length in order to prevent wide gaps at the ends of lines? (page 7:53)
- Are all paragraphs handled consistently, either indented or with the first lines of paragraphs following headings and subheadings flush left? (page 7:53)
- How are extracts indented: centered, or on one side only? (page 9:69)
- Are acronyms to be set in small capitals or in the uppercase of the typeface? (page 6:47)

The best way to handle this is to write your instructions clearly on the relevant pages of your manuscript, and then to prepare a separate *spec sheet* on which you list those same specifications so that your typesetter can refer to it if there is any doubt as to what you want done.

In addition, you should give the typesetter a copy of your house style guide. (page 9:78)

And don't forget to make an extra copy of your manuscript, with the latest corrections, before handing it to the typesetter, just in case something unthinkable happens to the original.

Another caution: Typing on a computer is not the same as typing on a typewriter. One mistake many computer beginners make is to tap the spacebar twice following a period at the end of a sentence, or after a colon. Since computers are programmed to take care of all word spacing, those extra spaces will be stretched beyond proportion when type is set justified. Enter only one space after a period or a colon.

A second mistake is to press the carriage return key at the end of a line, instead of allowing the computer to *wrap* automatically. The computer sees this as a *hard return*, causing the line always to break at that point. Use the carriage return key only to indicate the end of a paragraph.

Correcting the galleys

With the rapidly improving capabilities of computers, it is possible that the first set of proofs you see will be broken down into the actual pages, showing exactly where each page or chapter ends and where headings and subheadings will appear. This assumes that your pages consist of simple blocks of text, all uniform in appearance.

However, if your pages are more complex (as are the pages of this book), you may see only sheets of paper with continuous columns of text on them, with no indication of where the pages will break.

Either way, these are referred to as *proofs*, or *galleys* (named after the long narrow trays used to store metal type). Your job now is to read them carefully, looking for *typos* (typographical errors), or adjustments you want to make. This process is called *proofreading*, or simply *proofing*. It should not be confused with the term *copyediting*, which, as explained in the previous chapter, refers to the checking ("editing") of the manuscript ("copy") before it is set in type.

Do not do this entirely by yourself, especially if you wrote and typed the original manuscript. You know what you intended to type, and your eyes will often see it the way it should have been. Invariably, someone else will spot mistakes you cannot see.

The best way to proof a galley is to have two people

working on it at the same time. One will read aloud from the galley, specifying every punctuation mark and every new paragraph and spelling every proper name and every unusual word, while the other will follow along in the manuscript.

Don't rush the reading

At this stage the reading should not be rushed, but is better if done slowly and laboriously, with the two readers taking turns reading aloud. The better speller of the two should be the one to read the galleys, and even then extra care must be taken with words of unusual spelling. Keep your chosen dictionary close to hand, and do not be too proud, or too timid, to refer to it whenever in doubt.

If you do the proofing by yourself you should read aloud. This not only slows your pace but forces you to pay more attention to individual words. Many writers always read aloud what they have written in order to hear the rhythm of the sentences and the flow of the passages. The proofreading stage is the last chance you will have to do this before your words are forever captured on the printed page.

Use proofreader's marks

Corrections should be marked on the galleys, preferably with a red pencil or pen. There is a universal way of doing this, using a set of markings recognized by all typesetters. Some of the most commonly used symbols (or, *proofreader's marks*) are shown on the next page.

Be alert for errors that may have been created by entering computer codes incorrectly. For example, the code intended to close a quotation or to stop a run of italics may have been omitted.

If a piece of type looks cracked or broken, make a note to bring it to the attention of your typesetter. More than likely it is a fault on the proof copy only, but there is a possibility the actual type is at fault. Do not take chances. Let the typesetter check it again and, if necessary, correct it. Also, point out black spots or blotches on the page.

Corrections in margins

Make all corrections in the margins of the galley. Do not write in the body of text. Your typesetter will check

Proofreader's marks

To delete, put a slash through a singled character — or a line through several characters ~~characters~~ — and then place the delete sign in margin.

To restore deleted material, underline with dots and ~~then~~ write "stet" in margin.

Use a caret to indicate missing materal.

To insert a comma indicate the position with a caret then place this symbol in margin.

To insert an apostrophe where the typesetter didnt, use a caret and put this symbol in margin.

To insert a period, use a caret, with this mark in margin

To insert quotation marks, use carets within text and add symbols (quotes) in margin.

To insert space between words, use a slash (or caret) within the text, then place symbol in margin.

A new paragraph may be necessary. Mark the location and place symbol in margin.

If you need to run two paragraphs into one, indicate with line and add "no" to symbol in margin.

To spell out a number or an (abbrev.) word, circle the item and place an encircled "sp" in margin.

To change a Capital letter to lowercase, use a slash within text and write "lc" in margin.

To change lowercase letters to capitals — e.g., united states of America — use triple underlining and then write "caps" in margin.

To change regular capital letters to small capitals, as in acronyms (UNESCO, etc.), use double underlining and "sc" in margin.

To change regular type (roman) to italic, underline it once and write "ital" in margin.

To change italic type to regular type (roman), encircle it and write "rom" in margin.

To set as bold face, use a wavy line and write "bf" in margin.

the margins and may miss an alteration made only in the text. However, you will need to indicate where on the line of type the error or omission occurs. You do this with your colored pen or pencil by placing a caret (∧) where the insertion is to be made, or by drawing a single line through a word or letter to be deleted or corrected. Do not try to obliterate the words, or to make them illegible. Do not draw lines or arrows from within the text to the correction. These often tend to be more confusing than helpful. You can, however, draw a line with arrow when indicating the transposing of words within the text. Make sure it is clearly visible and not likely to be missed by the typesetter.

If you have several corrections on the same line, indicate them in their correct sequence (left to right) in the margin, separated by slanted lines.

When adding a long passage, you should type it on a separate piece of paper, mark it in some way (e.g., "insert A, line 5, galley 16") and attach it to the galley with a corresponding mark at the place where it is to be inserted — and remember to proof it carefully!

Spelling should be consistent

Check for consistency in the spelling of proper names and for capitalization of articles in titles.

Do not assume that the proofreading process can be handled entirely by a computer spell-check program. Your job can be made easier by running the text through one of these programs, but you still need to read all of it with your own eyes, paying careful attention to the SENSE of the words. For example, a spell-checker would not flag the last word in "Lady Godiva rode through Coventry on a white house."

It is a good idea to have someone read the galleys for content. When you are reading text slowly, concentrating on spelling and punctuation, you may not even realize that a passage does not make sense. It may have been poorly constructed in the first place, or a word may have been omitted when the original manuscript was typed. Before returning the corrected galleys to the typesetter, ask someone who has not already read it to read it now at a normal pace. Do not be surprised if that person spots something nobody else saw.

The typesetter will not charge for typographical errors, but you will have to pay for time involved in making all other corrections. That is why you need to indicate on the galleys which are your errors and which are the typesetter's. If yours, you write AA (*author's alteration*) in parentheses or a circle. If theirs, you write TE (*typographical error*) or PE (*printer's error* — a holdover from days when the typesetter worked for the printer).

When you have marked all the errors you can find, take the galleys back to the typesetter with the original manuscript, so that the typesetter can verify who pays for which corrections.

The revised proofs

After making the corrections, the typesetter will send you a second set of proofs (sometimes called *revised proofs*), along with the first set on which you made corrections. You must now check very carefully to make sure that all the corrections were in fact made, and that no other mistakes occurred during the process.

I assume your type is being set by computer, in which case you need check only the specific words or punctuation marked for correction. If the type is being set one line at a time on a linotype machine, you should check the lines immediately before and after lines containing corrections to make sure that no other mistakes were made when the original error was corrected.

Assuming that every letter and punctuation mark is now in its final position, you should be able to see where the word-breaks have fallen. After checking through all the corrections, and making any necessary notations, run your eye down the right-hand edge of the column of text to make sure that none of these corrections has created a bunch of new word-breaks farther down.

One final check

At the same time, look carefully at the spacing between the words and the letters. In trying to keep the number of word-breaks within your limitation, did the typesetter spread the text too much on the lines, or tighten it up too much?

If indeed all the pages are now complete, go through the whole book very carefully and make sure that the pages are numbered correctly, that captions are in the right places, and that all cross-references are where they should be. Some items may have been transferred unwittingly to a previous or following page when the adjoining text was reset.

Check page numbers in the table of contents and in the list of illustrations against the actual pages. Check page numbers in the index, especially if pages have been renumbered.

Check also that the text areas on facing pages are in alignment with one another.

Look at the typefaces. Have the correct ones been used for subheads, extracts, etc.?

What about the leading? Look carefully at spaces between lines and (if pertinent) between paragraphs, as well as the spaces above and below headings and subheadings. Are they consistent?

In the same way that you check the dictionary if you have the slightest doubt about the spelling of a word, so you should get out your type rule and check spacing that doesn't seem quite right. Maybe an extra line space has slipped in — or fallen out.

At this late stage changes can be expensive, and you may need to think twice about whether they are absolutely necessary. If they correct errors then of course the changes must be made. But if they are purely aesthetic, you should decide whether they justify the extra cost. Few writers can resist the temptation to move their own words around, but there comes a time when you have to say "Enough!"

On the next page is a check list to help remind you of some of the things to look for. Use the blank lines for reminders about points that apply specifically to your own book.

If you make any corrections on this second set of proofs, ask for another to see that they are carried out to your satisfaction.

The final set of proofs should be free of dirt and broken letters. Also, the inking throughout should be consistent. In other words, the density of the type should not vary from one page to another or — worse still — from one paragraph to another.

Checklist for final set of proofs

☐ Are all pages numbered correctly?

☐ Do all the captions appear in their proper places?

☐ Check all folios on the table of contents against the pages they refer to.

☐ Check all folios on the list of illustrations against the pages they refer to.

☐ Do the headings as listed on the table of contents match exactly those headings appearing in the book: same spelling, same punctuation, same capitalization, etc.?

☐ Check all cross-references in the book, making sure that the page numbers are correct.

☐ Check index items that may have been moved to new pages.

☐ If page numbers are included in the glossary, check those also.

☐ If text is ragged right, are you satisfied that there are no exceptionally wide gaps at the ends of the lines?

☐ If text is justified, are you satisfied with the word-breaks?

☐ Check the size and font of typefaces used for headings, subheadings, extracts, etc.

☐ Check the line spacing in text, and also around headings and subheadings.

☐ _____

☐ _____

☐ _____

☐ _____

☐ _____

20

Pasting up the boards

This chapter explains how to prepare your text for the printers by pasting it on boards. If the text has been set as complete pages — or if you are preparing and printing your book entirely on a computer — then you can skip this chaper and go to the next.

Preparing the mechanical

One of the first things the printers will do is photograph your pages onto film. Before that can be done, however, you (or your typesetter, or your production person) must provide *camera-ready artwork* — a pristine copy of all pages either as separate sheets (called *repros*, or reproduction proofs) or pasted down on thin cardboard (*boards*, or *mechanicals*).

Printers have their own ways of working, and you can save yourself money and time if you follow the particular procedures your printers use. Before going too far, ask a few basic questions such as:

- How should the artwork be prepared — as separate repros, or as pasteup mechanicals?
- If mechanicals, how should the pages be positioned — each page separately, two pages facing each other as they will finally appear in the book (4–5, 6–7, 8–9 etc.), or two pages facing each other as they will on the signature (4–17, 16–5, 6–15 etc.)?
- If two pages, should they butt each other, or should there be a 1" gap separating them?
- How should the positions of photographs or line illustrations be indicated — with *windows* (pieces of red film which, when exposed, will create black holes into which the image can be stripped), or with *keylines* (black outlines)?

If this process intimidates you, you could pay a production artist to do it for you. Check the yellow pages of your telephone directory (or *LMP*), under "graphic designers." These people charge either by the hour or by the project; in either case, because of the painstaking and time-consuming nature of the task, this service will not be cheap.

Tools of the trade

If you are going to prepare the boards yourself, you will need the following:

- a sturdy T-square
- a clear plastic triangle
- a steel ruler (better as a cutting edge than a wooden ruler)
- 2H or HB pencils (less likely to smudge or cut into the paper than softer or harder ones would)
- a kneaded eraser (it won't shed crumbs, which have a nasty habit of finding their way into the cement and under your pasteups)
- rubber cement and a thinning agent
- a long-necked container for the solvent
- a rubber cement pickup (since the rubber cement is toxic, this little eraser is preferable to rolling off the excess with your fingers)
- an electric waxer (instead of the rubber cement)
- masking tape
- cutting tools (an X-ACTO knife with spare blades, or a box of single-edged razor blades)
- a non-reproducible blue pencil (for writing instructions that can be seen by the printers but are not picked up by the camera)
- a drawing board (a large flat surface with straight edges for the T-square)
- a burnishing tool (a handy little gadget used to apply pressure when pasting down your artwork).

Ways to ensure uniformity

There are several ways you can ensure uniformity in preparing your mechanicals.

One way is to work on a *lightbox* (literally a box with a light inside it, and an opaque glass or plastic surface). A sheet of paper with your basic grid is taped to the surface, and your board is then taped securely on top of that so you can use the grid as a guide when positioning your text, running heads, folios, etc.

Another way is to draw the outline of the basic grid on every page separately, using a T-square, a triangle, and the non-reproducible blue pencil. You can paste your various pieces of type on top of that.

A third way is to use generic grid boards which you can buy at an art supply store (some printers will give you these if you ask). There are several variations on the market, most of them consisting of basic page formats with horizontal and vertical divisions which you can adapt to your specific layout. All you need do is attach your pieces of copy, using the blue lines as guides for true alignment.

You can also buy transparent overlay sheets with blue grid lines that are particularly handy for checking alignment on your mechanicals.

Make your own boards

However, the generic grid boards can prove expensive if you are working with a full-length book, and it may be cheaper — as well as more convenient — if you have your own printed.

Using your T-square, triangle, and a technical drawing pen, draw onto one of these generic boards a grid that will suit your specific needs. Indicate the basic trim-size of your page, and the exact location of your margins, running heads, image area, text area, etc.

If you want a grid that has several vertical and horizontal sections, enter these also. Add anything that is a constant on all of the pages.

Remember that the block of text on the left page may not appear in the same position as it does on the right page — that the two may use the grid differently. If this is the case, then you will have to make one plan for the verso and another for the recto.

Take these plans to a printer to have sufficient copies made on light-weight, smooth-surfaced boards. Tell the printer to use a non-reproducing blue ink.

But first: Find out how much the printer will charge for this, and then compare it with the cost of buying the same number of generic boards at the art supply store.

First, the dummy...

Before you work on the final pasteup you should famil-
iarize yourself with the procedure by making a *dummy*.
This is a rough replica of what your final book will look
like, showing exactly where the text ends on each page,
and how the illustrations look in position. It will also let
you know whether you'll have to juggle any pages to
make the whole thing fit. For example, do you need to
spread it out to avoid too many blanks at the back, or
close it up to get it all in?

The word *dummy* can also be a verb, so do not be confused if you hear of someone *dummying a page*.

First you will need an extra copy of the final proofs.
Either Xerox the copy you have or ask your typesetter
for a duplicate set, whichever way is cheaper. Then
you will need enough sheets of paper trimmed to the
actual size, or, preferably, to the size of a double
spread. If you are using pre-printed boards, you are
ready to start.

Cut out pieces of the photocopy as you need them and,
using your basic page grid as a guide, paste up each
page in turn.

If all your pages have the same amount of text appearing on them you need not do a complete dummy, but
just one for the front matter, the back matter, and a few
basic text pages and chapter openers.

It is a good idea to do another quick cast-off at this
point, before doing the final pasteup. Measure, in picas
or inches, how much text will fit on a page, and mark
off the pages on your galley. Pay attention to where the
illustrations and chapter openers fall. By numbering as
you go along you can see where you will need a blank
verso before starting a new chapter. Remember: All
even-numbered pages are verso and all odd-numbered
pages are recto.

...then the final boards!

The basic principle is the same when you work on the
final boards as when you worked on the dummy,
except that now you have to be especially careful in
everything you do.

If you use the lightbox technique, draw on a large sheet
of paper (or thin card) your basic double-page grid,

indicating the positions for text, running heads, folios, and possibly the chapter titles. The lines must be clear enough to be seen through the pasteup boards. Tape this to the surface of your lightbox, using your T-square and triangle to ensure that it is perfectly straight.

Now tape one of the pasteup boards on top of this, securing it so that it cannot move even a fraction of an inch; if it slips while you are working on it the error may show up in your printed page (one good reason to use pre-printed boards).

Cut text from the proofs as you need it, using either a pair of sharp scissors or a sharp blade against a metal ruler. Leave ⅛" on each side of the text. Coat the back either with rubber cement or on the electric waxer, and place it very carefully in position on the board. Before securing it, check with your T-square to make sure the lines are straight. With a large block of text you should use the triangle to check the edges. Or, use one of those transparent generic grid sheets. When you are satisfied the block is straight, place a clean piece of paper over it, and rub it down carefully with a burnishing tool.

If you use a one-coat cement you can lift and reposition each piece of paper until it is exactly where you want it. If necessary, squirt a small amount of solvent under the paper to loosen the glue.

Join text with care. When you have to join separate pieces of text together be very careful that you do not leave too much or too little space between them. Remember that the text is set with a very specific amount of leading between the lines, and you should not upset that now. When you have one page of the spread complete you should check with your T-square to see that the lines on the facing page are in alignment.

If your typesetter has given you all the corrections on separate galleys, without resetting them into the text, this is the time for you to make the adjustments. Note that the density of ink on these corrected pieces must be the same for all the surrounding text, or the difference will be noticeable when the pages are photographed by the printers.

If both the old and the new pieces are the same length, some people will simply paste the correction on top of the original. But this increases the thickness of the pasteup and, when photographed by the printer, can cause shadows (referred to as *cut lines*), which have to be deleted from the photographic plate by a process called *opaquing*. Some printers will charge the publisher for this. The best way is to very carefully cut out the mistake and replace it with the correction, making sure the thickness of the pasteup is consistent throughout.

White-out ink used on the boards can also create shadows, and should be used with care — or avoided.

Windows for artwork

If you have halftones, line drawings, or other artwork, you must indicate without any doubt exactly where they are to be placed. Either you draw a clear black frame, using a mechanical pen, or you cut and paste a *window* (a piece of red film) to cover the exact area.

If the frame is intended only as a position guide it should be ¹⁄₁₆" smaller on all sides, and marked "Position guide only. Do not print." If you want a line (*rule*) printed around the artwork you can have it either *flush* (touching all around), or with a gap, but in either case you must give very precise instructions such as: "Hairline rule flush all sides," or "¹⁄₁₆" gap all around."

In the middle of the frame you should write, in black ink, a code number or letter to identify that particular halftone or line drawing. Although the printers can see the code through the red window, the camera will see only a black hole into which the image will later be positioned (*stripped*).

As insurance against possible confusion, some publishers use *stats* (photostats) to identify exactly which photograph is to be used, and exactly how it is to be cropped/reduced/enlarged. This is called a *position stat*, and you should write across it the initials F.P.O. (for position only) to prevent its being mistaken for the final PMT.

Photostats can be made easily and inexpensively by most photocopying places.

Again, use the T-square and triangle to verify the precise position of each window.

If halftones or illustrations are to *bleed* (run off the page), the window or frame must extend ¹⁄₁₆" beyond the edge of the page.

➤ *See page 16:141 for more about bleeds.*

Inserting PMTs or Veloxes

Chapter 16 told how you can reproduce a photograph with either a PMT (Photomechanical Transfer) or a Velox, rather than go through the more costly process of making halftone negatives. If you are using this method, position the images very carefully and make sure they are perfectly straight on all sides. Mistakes made at this stage will show up on the printed pages of your book.

Keep it clean

When each page is complete, check and double-check it to make sure everything is in order. Cover the whole area with a piece of clean paper, turn it all over, and rub against it with the edge of your fist. Remove all dirty marks and fingerprints, and clean off all excess glue with the cement pickup, or a cotton swab soaked in a thinning agent. Make sure that no pieces of paper have curled up, and that no pieces of dirt are trapped beneath the type and creating mini-mountains that will cast shadows when photographed.

Do not paste the folio on the board yet. Wait until all the boards are done and you are quite sure you will not have to reshuffle any of the pages. However, the folio must be clearly marked on the board, either in non-reproducible blue within the page frame, or in pencil outside of it.

Check and double-check every page before moving on to the next one, watching for the many little things that can go wrong. On the next page is a checklist of some of the things to look for. Enter your own specific reminders in the blank lines.

Checklist for final pasteup

☐ Did any lines get left out at the top or bottom of pages, or when separate pieces were joined together?

☐ When separate pieces were joined together, were they the correct ones, or did you pick up a wrong piece?

☐ Is everything lying flat on the board — no curling or bumps?

☐ Are there any dirty marks, or creases, that will show up when photographed?

☐ Are there any widows at the tops of pages or columns?

☐ Are there any lonely subheads?

☐ In double-column text, are there any tombstones?

☐ Are captions in the right places?

☐ Do the lines of text align with those on facing pages?

☐ _____

☐ _____

☐ _____

☐ _____

21

Dealing with hardcovers

If you decide to do a hardcover edition there is a very specific set of decisions to make.

- How thick should the cover boards be?
- What material will you put on the boards?
- Do you need a jacket?
- What stamping on the spine?
- What endpapers?
- Do you want headbands?
- What stock to use for the dust jacket?

Cover boards

If you are using a reputable bindery you should be able to rely on their choice for the cover. For example, Thomson-Shore (considered one of the finest of short-run printers) uses .080" binder's boards for 5½" x 8½" and 6" x 9" books up to approximately 1" thick. When the book is thicker than 1" they use a heavier board (.088"), which they also use for all books measuring 7" x 10" or 8½" x 11". For exceptionally large, heavy books, they use either .095" or .100" boards.

What material for the boards?

You can cover the boards with either a cloth (grades A, B, or C) or a *non-woven vinyl*. You can also use a paper on the cover and have vinyl (or cloth) for the corners and spine. These materials come in a variety of colors and textures, so unless you have something specific in mind you may want to use what your printers have in stock without paying for a special order. When asking for an estimate of costs you can give a general indication, such as "B grade cloth."

As a rough guide, for a 6" x 9" book the A grade cloth

could cost you approximately 6 cents more per copy than if you used a non-woven vinyl (Kivar or Lexotone, for example); B grade cloth approximately 3 cents more than A grade cloth; and C grade cloth approximately 6 cents more than the B grade cloth.

When it comes time to select the color, choose carefully. Too many publishers, large and small, forget that this is another element in the overall design of a book, and they seem to be unaware of the jarring effect the color can have if it is not compatible with, say, the dust jacket. For a sense of unity you need to cover the boards with a color that either repeats or complements a major color on the jacket. Similar care should be taken when selecting the color of stamping, and the color of the endpapers, as is discussed later in this chapter.

The basic differences between the A, B, and C grades of cloth are the *thread count* and the durability, the C grade cloth being the most expensive and the one likely to last the longest, given normal wear and tear.

Who needs a jacket?

Not all hardcover books have jackets. Some have cover designs printed directly on the boards. This process can work out to be less expensive than using an A grade cloth with stamped spine and a separate laminated dust jacket. If interested, you should discuss this with your printer.

Spine stamping

There comes a time in the life of most case bound books when the jacket is discarded, at which point the only means of identification is what is stamped on the spine. Usually this consists of the book's title, the author's name (either in full or last name only), and the publisher's logo, imprinted in black, gold, or some other appropriate foil or color of ink.

The choice of typeface for this is important because in the foil stamping process the letters tend to merge, and the openings in characters such as *a*, *e*, and *g* become clogged, particularly if you have a heavily textured cover material. Be meticulous with your letter spacing here.

A touch of elegance can be added if you stamp something on the front board, even if it is only a symbol representing the book's theme (see Chapter 2), or — in the case of a biography — a handwritten signature.

And don't forget the obligatory Bookland bar code, or the ISBN, which should be placed on the back cover. If you do not have a jacket then one or the other of these symbols should be printed on the hardcover in the same position it would occupy on the jacket. If this is not practical, a printed, pressure-sensitive label should be affixed to the cover. Failing this, the code should be printed in the lower right corner of the inside back cover.

➤ *See Chapter 17 for more about the Bookland EAN code.*

Endpapers

The endpapers help to secure the cover boards to the book. At the front and the back of a book you will see that half of each sheet is glued to a board, and the other half is attached with a thin line of glue to the outer signature.

Many publishers use one of the heavy papers normally used for covers and dust jackets, but there is a paper designed specifically for this purpose. It has a unique built-in folding strength and costs a few cents more per copy than the regular cover papers. Ask your printer about availability.

Keep in mind that this is another element of design. Select a texture and color that will complement the cloth or vinyl on the cover as well as the colors of the jacket. If it is not colored it should match or blend comfortably with the paper used for the book's pages. For example, if the pages are a warm natural white do not select a brilliant white for the endpapers.

Headbands

At the top and the bottom of the spine on well-made case bound books you will see small strips of colored cords. These are known as *headbands,* and their sole function is to help prevent damage when a person tugs on a spine while pulling a book off a tightly packed shelf.

If you decide to include them in your book's spine, and you have a choice of colors, you should keep in mind the colors surrounding them on the jacket and on the material covering the boards.

The dust jacket

Your printers will need to know what thickness of paper you want for the dust jacket. Probably the most popular choice is a white stock that is .010" thick and coated on one side. This is referred to as 10pt CIS. A slightly more expensive and thicker sheet, known as 12pt CIS, is also available.

22

Requesting a quotation

While your text is being set you should be looking for a printer to bring it all together as a finished book. As I mentioned earlier, you will find a list of printers in *Literary Market Place*. To help you select the ones to write to, study John Kremer's *Directory of Book, Catalog, and Magazine Printers,* which is based on the experiences and comments of hundreds of small independent publishers.

Len Fulton conducted a similar survey which was published in *Small Press Review* in February 1988.

➤ *See Appendix A for a list of major short-run printers.*

Many popular short-run printers are in Michigan. Their prices are more competitive than those on the West Coast, partly because of their proximity to paper mills. And, since most of them have been catering to small publishers for many years, they are especially sensitive to your needs.

Nevertheless, there are a number of very fine printers on the West Coast and you should include a selection in your mailing.

Choose at least half a dozen printers and send each one of them a Request for Quotation form with specific details of what you want. Most printers can supply you with copies of their own forms, but if you want to get a fair comparison you need to provide exactly the same specifications to each printer and you can do this only if you have an identical form for all of them.

On the next page is the form I used when seeking a printer for this book, and in Appendix A is a larger version you can duplicate after adding your own name and address.

Company: _____

Street: _____ City: _____ State: _____ Zip: _____

Telephone: (____) _____ Fax: (____) _____

Contact person: _____ Position: _____

REQUEST FOR QUOTATION

Date of this request: _____ Books needed by (date): _____

Book title: _____

Trim size: _____ No. of pages: _____

Quantity: _____

Additional 100s: _____

Text paper: 50-lb. ❑   55-lb. ❑   60-lb. ❑   other (specify): _____
              white ❑   natural ❑   other (specify): _____

Binding: casebound ❑   paperback ❑   Smyth sewn ❑
           perfect bound ❑   saddlestitch ❑   other (specify): _____

Cover stock: _____

Cover coating: _____

Cover ink: 1 color ❑   2 colors ❑   other (specify): _____

Jacket stock: _____

Jacket coating: _____

Jacket ink: 1 color ❑   2 colors ❑   other (specify): _____

No. of halftones: _____

Material provided: _____

Proofs/bluelines: _____

Estimated freight charges: _____

Other requirements: _____

_____

Filling out this form will force you to make certain decisions you may have been procrastinating over.

When do you want the books?
Most printers need 5–6 weeks to produce a standard paperback, and 8–10 weeks for a hardcover. Their busiest times are summer and fall, when publishers are clamoring to get their books out in time for Christmas. Let the printers know if you need your book by a certain date. Sometimes they can give it priority, but you will have to pay rush charges for the privilege.

With careful planning you can save money by having your book printed early in the year. Several printers offer discount prices during March, April, and May when their business is slack. When you send in your request form ask if they offer such a discount and, if so, during which months.

Trim size
This should be easy: It was one of the first decisions you made when designing the book. Remember that the first figure should be the width and the second the height. If you reverse them, and the printer misunderstands your needs, the quotation will be useless.

➤ *See Chapter 2.*

Number of pages
Chapter 10 describes how you can estimate the number of pages your book will need to accommodate your manuscript. By now you should be able to make a more accurate guess.

Quantity
Most short-run printers can print any quantity of books from 100 to 10,000. However, most small publishers think in terms of 1,000 to 2,000 copies. You will hear people say that the more copies you print the less you pay for each copy. This is true — if you sell all your books. However, I know of several publishers whose living rooms are cluttered with cartons of books that were printed two or three or more years ago. If they divide the number of copies sold into the total cost of printing, the reality is that each book cost several times the price it sold for. Be realistic when estimating how many you will need.

Unless you have a firm order for copies from a distributor or are reasonably certain you can sell a vast quantity through direct mail or by some other means, you should be conservative rather than adventurous with your first print order.

According to Ned Thomson of Thomson-Shore, Inc., there are no specific price breaks when it comes to figuring the cost of printing. He says that virtually all the set-up costs are charged to the first fifty or so copies, adding:

> That first fifty copies may cost $1,000 and every additional copy, up to 5,000 or so, could be 75 cents each. Under that formula, the first 500 copies would cost approximately $1,375 or $2.75 each, 1,000 copies would be $1,750 or $1.75 each, 2,000 would be $2,500 or $1.25 each and 5,000 would be $4,075 or 95 cents each. There is no specific point where prices drop but, if you graphed it, the line curves gently downward as quantities increase.

To help you decide how many copies to order, and to find out how much each copy will cost, ask for a quote on several different quantities, such as 1,000, 1,500 and 2,000 copies, and then ask how much each additional 100 will cost.

Because the book goes through several different operations during its production, the printer usually starts out with enough paper to print 10% to 12% more copies than you have ordered. A number of copies may be spoiled and discarded as the different machines are being set up. The theory is that by the end of the operation there will be the number you requested. However, sometimes there are fewer copies and sometimes more. In the printing industry there is a set of Trade Customs, one of which states:

> Over runs or under runs not to exceed 10% on quantities ordered, or the percentage agreed upon, shall constitute acceptable delivery. The printer will bill for actual quantity delivered within this tolerance. If customer requires quaranteed exact quantities, the percentage tolerance must be doubled.

Reputable printers will charge you only for the actual numbers they ship to you, and they will indicate the correct number on your final invoice.

If you need a specific number of books you should inform the printers when placing your order.

Text paper

The question of paper is so complex that I am devoting a full chapter (Chapter 23) to it. Study it before making up your mind. For now, here are a few generalities.

Most printers maintain a supply of certain papers that they buy in huge quantities These are referred to as their *house papers,* or *inventory stock.* They come in 50-lb, 55-lb and 60-lb weights, usually in shades of white or natural. The white papers are smooth and approximately 10% cheaper than the natural papers, which tend to be more opaque. Natural papers have a higher bulk than white papers, which means they will make your book thicker. If your book is heavily illustrated you should consider a coated paper, either for the whole book or for the separate signatures that contain photographs.

It seems that small independent publishers have established a vanguard in the swing to acid-free papers, while major publishing houses continue to print books that can be guaranteed to disintegrate within 35 or 50 years. Nearly all short-run printers carry a good variety of acid-free papers that do not cost much more than the acidic ones.

The most economical way of selecting a paper is to ask the printers to give you a quote on, for example, "60-lb natural book paper," and request they let you know what that paper will be, preferably with a sample. If you have a specific paper in mind, such as "80-lb Mohawk Superfine softwhite-smooth," you should request it by its full name and then add "or equivalent." When the bids come back, check to make sure the printers have identified what the paper is.

➤ *See Chapter 23 for more about paper.*

Binding

The difference in cost between hardcover and paperback will depend on several variables. As a very rough guide you can expect to pay at least $1 more per copy for 1,500 6" x 9" 256-page hardcover books than for 1,500 of the same books paperbound. The difference for 1,500 8½" x 11" 256-page books would be at least $1.50 per copy.

The only way you can find out how much your book will cost is to submit your specifications to printers. If you cannot make up your mind about which way to go, ask for three prices: (1) if the book is hardcover, (2) if the book is paperback, and (3) if the printing is split, with so-many hardcover and so-many paperback.

➤ *See Chapter 2 for more about methods of binding.*

Stock for cover or jacket
Most publishers choose a white stock that is .010" thick and coated on one side (10pt C1S) for covers or jackets. Another choice is slightly thicker — 12pt C1S. The coating is not applied on the reverse side because the glue that binds the pages to the cover would not adhere to it.

➤ *See Chapter 17 for more about protective coatings.*

Material provided
If you have all your pages laid out on boards, with halftones made to size and everything ready for the printers to photograph, then you can say you are providing "camera-ready artwork." If you want the printers to make the halftone negatives for you, say so on the request form.

Proofs/bluelines
Printers prepare their own set of proofs before doing a book. This way they can make sure that everything is as it should be — that the pages are in their right order, that margins are correct, and that all stripped-in artwork is positioned properly. It is the last chance before the presses roll. It is now or never.

Because these proofs are usually printed with a blue ink they are referred to as *blues,* or *bluelines.*

Printers will show these to a publisher — for a fee — at the same time warning that any corrections the publisher makes at this late stage could be expensive and delay the book's production. You will be charged about 40–60 cents per page, depending upon the method your printers use to produce them.

The question of whether or not to see them should be based on the type of book you are printing. If it is one of straight text, and all pages are very similar in layout, an abbreviated set of blues (say, of one signature only) will let you check if the pages are lined up correctly. If the book is heavily illustrated with halftones or other stripped-in artwork, you should check a full set of blues just to make sure these appear in their correct positions, with appropriate captions.

A check copy. Instead of a set of blues, some printers offer to send you a *check copy* of all the pages after they have been printed and before they are bound. Any corrections you request at this stage will, of course, be very costly, although the printers will absorb the cost of correcting any mistakes they have made. Ask your printers if they provide this option.

If you do decide to see blues you should study them and return them within 24 hours to avoid any further delay in the production of your book.

It shouldn't take too long to check the blueline of a 320-page book. Rather than try to see everything at once, it is better to run through three times. First, check the margins to see that they are even, and that the pages are aligned correctly and in their proper sequence. Next, check illustrations to see that they are in their right places, that they have the right captions, and that they have not been *flopped* (that is, printed backward or upside down).

Finally, go through the pages slowly, looking for broken letters, specks of dirt, and flaws of any sort which might be on the negative and eventually appear on the pages of your book. Mark any you find, to bring them to the attention of your printers.

This is not a time to look for typographical errors, or to add or delete text. You should have taken care of all those matters before sending everything to the printers.

A separate proof is made of the cover or jacket.

Indicate on your request form whether you want to see full blues or only the first signature. If you are still undecided, you could ask for the cost of each to be separated from the estimate's total.

Freight charges

Many beginning publishers forget that their books have to be shipped from the printers, sometimes across the entire continent, and they are shocked when the bill comes in from the freight company. It could run into hundreds of dollars. To avoid this embarrassment, ask for an estimate.

Extra jackets for promotion

Almost all major publishers have extra copies of the jacket or cover printed long before a book is complete, and their sales representatives use these when selling to bookstores. The stores want to know what a book will look like on their shelves and tables, so these extra jackets become a vital sales tool.

Many small publishers use a similar technique, except that they usually mail the extra jackets, or covers, with other promotional material. Some take them to a local printer and have pertinent information printed on the reverse — the price, a synopsis, how the book can be ordered, etc.

If you decide to go this route, use the "other requirements" line to ask for the cost of an extra supply of covers or jackets.

23

A paper primer

Paper is probably the most expensive item in the production of a book, and selecting the right paper is as crucial as selecting the right typeface. In both instances the criterion should be APPROPRIATENESS.

A bright white paper may be suitable for a manual or a scholarly reference book — cold and factual — whereas a warm, *natural* paper would be more appropriate for the sort of book your readers will want to curl up with.

A glossy paper may be ideal for reproducing photographs but it can be too glaring for a long, continuous reading of text. A dull paper can rob photographs of their brilliance.

If the paper is too thin the print will show through from the other side. This is referred to as *show through*. It is not a problem if the blocks of text are the same size and in the same position on each page, but it can be very distracting if you have heavy type on pages that back onto line drawings or semi-blank pages.

But paper can also be too thick. If too bulky it could make your book heavier than you would like it to be, adding to the cost of shipment.

Paper is stock, stock is paper
The word *stock* is often used as a generic term for paper. It does not refer necessarily to papers your printer has "in stock." Those are variably called *house papers, inventory stock*, or *papers on the floor*.

Acid-free papers
One of your first decisions should be whether to use an *acid-free* paper. This boils down to the question "Do

you want the book to last longer than, say, 35 years, without its pages changing color, becoming brittle, and disintegrating?"

Pages from Gutenberg's Bible are almost as pristine today as when they came off his press in the year 1456, yet the pages of books printed during the past hundred years are crumbling on their shelves. This is happening to more than one-third of all the books in the Library of Congress.

The difference is in our modern technology. One of the compounds used in making paper from wood contains an acid which, over time, eats into the fibers, causing the paper to disintegrate. Although this fact became known many years ago, paper mills have been slow to change their methods of production. The new, acid-free papers were expensive, and major publishers refused to use them. University presses, independent presses, and adventurous self-publishers eventually formed a vanguard in publishing books guaranteed to last hundreds of years.

Cost is no longer an issue. Today the price differential between acid-free and acidic papers is less significant, and there is on the market a greater variety of papers to choose from.

Libraries prefer books that are printed on acid-free paper, so if you decide to use it you should say so in your promotional material.

In 1984 The American National Standards Institute established the criteria for permanence of uncoated paper and recommended the following notice be printed on the copyright page of all books made with approved acid-free paper:

 The paper used in this publication meets the minimum requirements of the American National Standard for Information Sciences — Permanence of Paper for Printed Library Materials, ANSI Z39.48-1984.

The symbol is the mathematical infinity symbol set inside a circle.

If your book is printed on acid-free paper notify the Library of Congress when you apply for your CIP data and they will add the abbreviation "alk. paper" — as you can see on page 12:102.

Color of paper

Not all white papers are the same color. Some have a subtle blue cast, creating a bright white surface that is popular for reference books and manuals, and for other scholarly books. *Natural* papers come in warmer shades of white, off-white, or cream. These are preferable for novels and some non-fiction books.

If you have halftones you should bear in mind that they will be affected by the color of the stock: The whites in the photographic images will be only as white as the surface of the paper.

Basis weight

Different papers are made for different applications. *Bond* papers are intended for stationery, business forms, and leaflets, and are generally the ones you'll find at your local print shops. *Newsprint* is used for newspapers. *Book* and *text* papers are used for the pages of books (*text* is an abbreviation of *texture* and does not refer to printed text). *Cover stocks* are used for book covers.

Some standard sizes are:

- bond paper = 17" x 22"
- newsprint = 24" x 36"
- book and text papers = 25" x 38"; 23" x 29"
- cover stock = 20" x 26".

The papers in each category are graded according to their *basis weight*, which is the weight of one ream (500 sheets). Until you are used to it, this method can be confusing, especially if you hold in one hand a piece of 60-lb book stock and in your other hand a piece of 60-lb cover stock, and you can feel that one is heavier than the other. The point to remember is that sheets in one ream measured 20" x 26", while sheets in the other measured 25" x 38".

It is rather like comparing apples with oranges, but that is the way it is done in the United States. Other countries have a metric system which determines the *grammage* (number of grams per square meter) for all categories of paper.

Most books are printed on either 50-lb, 55-lb, or 60-lb book stock, and most covers are printed on either 50-lb, 65-lb, or 80-lb cover stock.

Opacity

As I mentioned at the beginning of this chapter, you should avoid allowing the print on one side of a page to show through to the other side, particularly if you have line drawings or halftones in the book. So you should consider the *opacity* of the paper: How opaque is it? One way to test this is to lay a sheet of paper on top of a printed surface. If the *show through* is only slight it may be acceptable, but if it is too obvious you should try another stock.

As a general rule, you will find that light-weight uncoated stocks (50-lb, 55-lb, etc.) will be less opaque than heavy coated ones (65-lb, 70-lb, etc.).

Surface

The surface of a paper will affect how the type appears on the page. On uncoated stock the ink will sink into the fibers and, depending on the coarseness of the surface, may give jagged edges to individual letters. Except in extreme cases, this is acceptable for many categories of books. In fact, this is how it was in the days of hand-set type, when there were no smooth coated papers.

A coated matte sheet feels smooth when you run your fingers across it, and type will look clean because it is not being absorbed by the paper but is sitting on top of the surface. This paper is more expensive than uncoated paper but has the added advantage of being suitable for halftones as well as for text.

A step higher on the scale is the enamel coated sheet. This is what most people think of when they talk about *coated* papers. It has a high gloss and a hard, smooth surface. It will give a much better rendering of halftones and is essential when reproducing color photographs. Because glue won't adhere to the coating, these sheets cannot be used in a perfect bound book.

Bulk and PPI

Another term you may hear used is *bulk*. This refers to the thickness of the paper and is usually rated in PPI (pages per inch). Generally you can assume that the heavier papers are bulkier than lighter ones. But you should also take into account a paper's surface. A rough-surface, uncoated paper will have greater bulk than a smooth-surface paper, although one with a heavy enamel coating may be even thicker.

All of this comes into play when you need to determine the thickness of your book. If your manuscript is short and requires, for example, only 96 pages, you can make the book bigger by using a thicker paper, thus justifying the price you are selling it for.

Alternatively, if it is a big book already you may run into problems at the bindery. Most perfect binding machines are limited to books up to 1¾" thick, and case binding machines to 2½". In these cases you would use a stock that has less bulk. Bibles and dictionaries are good examples.

Grain

Most paper is made from wood, the fibers of which run in a direction determined by the flow of the paper-making machine. This direction is referred to as the paper's *grain*. In some papers the grain runs along the length of the sheet (*grain long*) while in others it runs across the width (*grain short*).

A book should be bound so that its spine aligns with the grain. Otherwise the pages will not lie flat but will curl inward from top to bottom. Generally this is an area you need not be concerned with because — we hope — you are dealing with reputable printers who know exactly what is required.

The question of grain will be important when you are designing and printing promotional brochures and fliers at your local print shop, where the printers may not always be as judicious.

The point to remember is that paper will fold more easily and lie flatter when folded WITH THE GRAIN than when folded AGAINST THE GRAIN. To see how this works, take a sheet of paper and tear it, first from top to bottom, then from left to right. One of the tears will be rough, running off in a diagonal direction, while the other will be fairly straight. The jagged tear is made against the grain, and the straight one is with the grain.

If you fold the sheet from top to bottom, and from side to side, the fold made with the grain will have a sharp crease, while the one made against it will be jagged, possibly revealing some of the tiny chips of wood.

At your local print shop make sure your promotional piece is printed on paper with the grain corresponding to the direction in which you want to fold it.

Paper samples

Most printers or paper suppliers will be pleased to give you samples of their house papers so that you can select the ones most appropriate for your book. In some cases the samples come bound as small books with text and halftones printed on them.

Once you have narrowed your choice to one or two papers, you might be able to get a *dummy* from either the paper supplier or the printing company. This is a book of blank pages trimmed (and sometimes bound) to the exact size of your book.

Check your telephone directory to see if you have any paper suppliers in your area and, if so, call and talk to the samples department. This way you can get an idea of what you want before you write to printers requesting their quotes.

Costs and availability

In the early days of computers people said we would soon need less and less paper, and that entire forests would be spared. Some people even predicted a paperless world. In reality, just the opposite has happened. The demand for paper is greater than ever. Not only are office printers churning out thousands of documents and millions of pieces of junk mail each year, but a whole new genre of magazines and books has been born.

With competition growing, each of these entities has called for better quality papers, with a special emphasis on the high-gloss sheets, thus creating a backlog of orders at the mills. For this reason, if you want enamel coated stock for your book you should seek a printer as early as possible and get your order in. Otherwise, you may find your book will be delayed several weeks.

24

The final stages

Now for the final steps — sending the camera-ready artwork to the printers, checking the bluelines, and waiting for the books to arrive.

Do not send ANYTHING to the printers until you can send EVERYTHING. In other words, if your index is not yet complete, don't send the rest of the pages and say "the index is coming."

What to send

Carefully pack your mechanicals or camera-ready pages in a box, or tape them securely between two pieces of thick cardboard. Enclose all pieces of artwork such as photographs or line drawings. It is a good idea to send the dummy you made when pasting up the layouts if you have a lot of halftones or other stripped-in artwork.

Put as much as possible in writing to avoid misunderstanding. This is best done with a specification sheet on which you list your instructions for the job. Be sure to point out any changes from the original request. Include a detailed pagination sheet listing the correct sequence of pages, and be sure to indicate where the blank pages fall.

This is the time to clarify issues that weren't completely resolved when you mailed the Request for Quotation, such as how you want the books shipped to you, and how many extra covers or dust jackets you want for publicity purposes.

Who owns the negatives?

The printers make negatives of your artwork in order to make plates for the press. The question of who owns these negatives is a delicate one, and there is a difference of opinion. According to Ned Thomson, in book printing the publisher is considered the owner, even though some printers offer to store negatives for the publishers. In the general printing industry, however, it seems that the printers claim ownership.

What you need to make clear in the beginning is whether or not you want the negatives and, if so, whether they should be sent to you or stored by the printers. Make a note of this on the specification sheet you send in with the artwork.

Looking ahead to a reprint. The issue revolves around the possibility that at some time in the future you will want to print another edition. If the same printers are going to do the reprint they should retain the negatives. If you think you may go elsewhere, then these negatives should be sent to you and stored in a suitable place — ideally they should be kept flat, and in an air-conditioned environment.

You may run into problems when asking one printing company to work with negatives made by another unless the two companies have very similar methods of working. In the end you may be better off letting the new printers make a fresh set of negatives.

Return of artwork

Do not assume that the printers will automatically return all your artwork. Some do, some do not. Indicate your preference on the *spec sheet*.

Keep a copy of everything

Before sending your package to the printers make photocopies of everything, including your instructions, so that if you receive a phone call a week later asking what you mean on page such-and-such you will know exactly what the printers are looking at.

Although no one likes to think such things will happen, your package could get lost en route, the plane could crash, or the printing plant could go up in flames. At least if you have a photocopy you can reconstruct the artwork, so your efforts over all these months, or years, will not have been for naught.

Insure everything for full replacement value.

When the books arrive

The doorbell rings, and you see a huge truck in your driveway.

Your books have arrived!

The back of the truck is rolled up and you see dozens of cartons strapped together on a pallet. Then the driver turns to you and asks, "Where's your fork-lift?"

Despite all your other carefully laid plans, this is probably one question you had not anticipated.

But this great moment of your life — when your first books arrive — need not be marred by trauma.

Discuss with your printers what options you have concerning the number of books that can be packed in each carton, and how many cartons there will be. Just remember, you will probably be the one carrying those cartons around. Also, find out whether the stacks of cartons will be wrapped in plastic or bound with metal bands.

Make sure all this is indicated on your spec sheet so there is no confusion later.

And plan to have extra pairs of strong and willing hands nearby when that truck arrives, because some drivers may tell you their responsibility ends at your front door, or at the tailgate of the truck.

Save the pallet

It is always a good idea to store cartons of books off the ground, particularly if you are keeping them in a garage or other cement-covered area. My final piece of advice to you is to ask for the pallet from the truck and to use it to stack your cartons of books on — though I trust they won't be in storage for long.

Besides, the pallet will come in handy for your next book, too.

GOOD LUCK!

III

APPENDICES

Appendix A

Short-run printers

Here are a few printers you can approach for a short-run printing. For a more comprehensive list see Literary Market Place. *However, for a truly in-depth overview of services offered by printers you may want to study John Kremer's* Directory of Book, Catalog, and Magazine Printers *(Ad-Lib Publications, P.O. Box 1102, Fairfield, IA 52556-1102). In it, printers are compared according to their prices and their services, based on surveys Kremer conducted among small publishers.*

On the next page is a Request for Quotation form which you can photocopy. Use it as it is, or block out the upper section and insert your own letter-head and logo.

➤ *See Chapter 22 for help when submitting a request.*

Bertelsmann Printing & Manufacturing Corp.
1021 Stannage Avenue, Albany, CA 94706
Tel: (415) 527-4514

BookCrafters
613 E. Industrial Drive, P.O. Box 370, Chelsea, MI 48118-0370
Tel: (313) 475-9145

Braun-Brumfield, Inc.
P.O. Box 1203, Ann Arbor, MI 48106-1203
Tel: (313) 662-3291

Delta Lithograph Co.
28210 N. Avenue Stanford, Valencia, CA 91355
Tel: (805) 257-0584; California (800) 223-1478; nationwide (800) 32DELTA

Edwards Brothers Inc.
2500 South State Street, P.O. Box 1007, Ann Arbor, MI 48106
Tel: (313) 769-1000

Griffin Printing & Lithograph Co. Inc.
544 W. Colorado Street, Glendale, CA 91204
Tel: (213) 245-3671; (818) 244-2128; California (800) 423-5789; nationwide (800) 826-4849

GRT Book Printing
3960 East 14th Street, Oakland, CA 94601
Tel: (415) 534-5032

Malloy Lithographing, Inc.
5411 Jackson Road, P.O. Box 1124, Ann Arbor, MI 48106
Tel: (313) 665-6113

McNaughton & Gunn Inc.
P.O. Box 2070, Ann Arbor, MI 48106
Tel: (313) 429-5411

Spillman Printing
1801 Ninth Street, P.O. Box 340219, Sacramento, CA 95834
Tel: (916) 448-3511; nationwide (800) 448-3511

Thomson-Shore, Inc.
7300 West Joy Road, P.O. Box 305, Dexter, MI 48130-0305
Tel: (313) 426-3939

Company: _____

Street: _____ City: _____ State: _____ Zip: _____

Telephone: (_____) _____ Fax: (_____) _____

Contact person: _____ Position: _____

REQUEST FOR QUOTATION

Date of this request: _____ Books needed by (date): _____

Book title: _____

Trim size: _____ No. of pages: _____

Quantity: _____

Additional 100s: _____

Text paper: 50-lb. ❑   55-lb. ❑   60-lb. ❑   other (specify): _____

       white ❑   natural ❑   other (specify): _____

Binding: casebound ❑   paperback ❑   Smyth sewn ❑

       perfect bound ❑   saddlestitch ❑   other (specify): _____

Cover stock: _____

Cover coating: _____

Cover ink: 1 color ❑   2 colors ❑   other (specify): _____

Jacket stock: _____

Jacket coating: _____

Jacket ink: 1 color ❑   2 colors ❑   other (specify): _____

No. of halftones: _____

Material provided: _____

Proofs/bluelines: _____

Estimated freight charges: _____

Other requirements: _____

_____

_____

Appendix B

Schools and classes

Here are a few of the institutions and associations that sponsor classes related to book design and/or production. A more comprehensive list can be found in Literary Market Place.

Association of the Graphic Arts
The Evening School
5 Penn Plaza, 20th floor, New York, N.Y. 10001
Tel: (212) 279-2100
Director: Gail C. Zambrano
Classes held in Long Island, Manhattan, Westchester, and New Jersey.

The City University of New York, Graduate Center
Education in Publishing Program
33 West 42nd Street, New York, N.Y. 10036-8099
Tel: (212) 642-2910

Dynamic Graphics Educational Foundation
Visual Communication Workshops
6000 North Forest Park Dr., P.O. Box 1901,
Peoria, IL 61656-1901
Tel: (309) 688-8866; (800) 255-8800

Hofstra University
1000 Fulton Avenue, Hempstead, N.Y. 11550
Tel: (516) 560-5454
Robert B. Sargent, Chairman, English Dept.

New York University, Center for Publishing
School of Continuing Education
48 Cooper Square, New York, N.Y. 10003
Tel: (212) 998-7219
Director: Ronald W. Janoff

Otis Art Institute of Parsons School of Design
2401 Wilshire Blvd., Los Angeles, CA 90057
Tel: (213) 251-0505

Parsons School of Design
Div. of The New School
66 West 12th Street, New York, N.Y. 10011
Tel: (212) 741-8910

Rochester Institute of Technology
School of Printing Management & Sciences
One Lomb Memorial Drive, P.O. Box 9887,
Rochester, N.Y. 14623-0887
Tel: (716) 475-5484
Director: Mark F. Guldin

School of Visual Arts
Office of Continuing Education
209 East 23rd Street, New York, N.Y. 10010
Tel: (212) 683-0600
Director: Anthony P. Rhodes

Stanford Publishing Course, Stanford University
Stanford Alumni Association
Bowman Alumni House, Stanford, CA 94305
Tel: (415) 725-1083

University of California Extension
Certificate Program in Publishing
2223 Fulton Street, Berkeley, CA 94720
Tel: (415) 642-4231

The University of Chicago
Publishing Program
5835 S. Kimbark Avenue, Chicago, IL 60637
Tel: (312) 702-1722

Appendix C

Stock photo sources

Here are a few sources you can approach for stock photographs. The first four are commercial companies that will charge you according to how the photos are used and how many copies of the book are being printed. The other four are government agencies that will usually charge you only the cost of producing the actual prints. In each case you should be as precise as possible when making a request. State specifically what it is you want, and how you will be using it. Some places charge a search fee. A more comprehensive list can be found in Literary Market Place.

➤ *See* **Using stock photos,** *Chapter 17.*

COMMERCIAL SOURCES:

Bettmann
The Bettmann Archive; Bettman Newsphotos
902 Broadway, New York, N.Y. 10010
Tel: (212) 533-4034
Contact: David Greenstein
More than 25 million images, from ancient cave paintings to today's news photographs. Bettmann houses the complete photo libraries of United Press International and Reuters, covering virtually every significant event and personality of the twentieth century.

Comstock, Inc.
30 Irving Place, New York, N.Y. 10003
Tel: (212) 353-8600; (800) 225-2727
Executive Director, Editorial: Jane S. Kinne
Photos of children, food, industrial interiors, international travel, people, natural history, science, scenics, sports, transportation.
Comstock Desktop Photography now offers images on CD-ROM disks.

Culver Pictures Inc.
150 W 22nd Street, New York, N.Y. 10011
Tel: (212) 645-1672
Contact: Stevie Holland
A large historical collection of portraits, movie stills, inventions, science, sports, theater, etc., to World War II and the 1950s.

Wide World Photos, Inc.
Subsidiary of the Associated Press
50 Rockefeller Plaza, New York, N.Y. 10020
Tel: (212) 621-1940
Director: Patricia Lantis
More than 50 million images: historical, news, celebrities, sports.

NON-COMMERCIAL SOURCES:

Library of Congress
Photoduplication Service
Washington, D.C. 20540
Tel: (202) 287-5640
Black and white prints of material housed in the Library of Congress, including millions of books, pamphlets, historic documents, and photographs. Minimum cost of an 8" x 10" reproduction: $7 for "regular printing" and $26 for "exhibition quality printing."

NASA
Audio Visual Section
400 Maryland Ave. SW, Washington D.C. 20546
Tel: (202) 453-8375
Color transparencies and black and white prints of astronauts, space flights, and space explorations are available free of charge to "information media," according to a note in the *NASA Photography Index.* That includes book publishers.

National Archives and Records Administration
The Still Picture Branch (NNSP)
Washington, D.C. 20408
Tel: (202) 523-3236
Reference: Fred Pernell
Four million pictures from the files of numerous
U.S. federal government agencies. If you know
exactly what you want you can order through the
mail. Or you can make an appointment to visit,
and look through the files without charge. An
8" x 10" print will cost about $6.

United States Naval Institute
The Photo Library
Annapolis, MD 21402
Tel: (301) 268-6110
Photographs of ships and aircraft of the U.S.
Navy and Coast Guard, as well as of the other
services; weapons; combat; military person-
alities. Also photos of foreign navies and military
personnel.

Recommended reading

These books are categorized according to their principal topic. Some could overlap into more than one category, and a few could be listed in all categories. Do not limit yourself to this list. Visit art supply stores regularly to check their bookshelves for the latest arrivals.

The bibliography that follows this list encompasses a much wider range of books about books, many of which are not included here either because they are not related to design and production or because they are not easy to locate.

Design and layout

BOOK DESIGN AND MANUFACTURE—Vincent Blyden. Graphic Arts Technical Foundation, 4615 Forbes Avenue, Pittsburgh, PA 15213-3796.

COMPLETE GUIDE TO ILLUSTRATION AND DESIGN TECHNIQUES AND MATERIALS—Terence Dalley, editor. Chartwell Books Inc., 110 Enterprise Avenue, Secaucus, N.J. 07094.

DESIGN OF BOOKS, THE—Adrian Wilson. Peregrine Smith Books, P.O. Box 667, Layton, UT 84041.

DO-IT-YOURSELF GRAPHIC DESIGN—John Laing. Macmillan Publishing Company, 866 Third Avenue, New York, N.Y. 10022.

EDITING BY DESIGN—Jan V. White. R.R. Bowker Company, 1180 Avenue of the Americas, New York, N.Y. 10036.

FUNDAMENTALS OF LAYOUT—F.H. Wills. Dover Publications Inc., 180 Varick Street, New York, 10014.

GRID, THE—Allen Hurlburt. Van Nostrand Reinhold Company, 135 West 50th Street, New York, N.Y. 10020.

HOW TO UNDERSTAND AND USE DESIGN AND LAYOUT— Alan Swann. North Light Books, F & W Publications Inc., 1507 Dana Avenue, Cincinnati, OH 45207.

LAYOUT: THE DESIGN OF THE PRINTED PAGE—Allen Hurlburt. Watson-Guptill Publications, 1515 Broadway, New York, N.Y. 10036.

METHODS OF BOOK DESIGN—Hugh Williamson. Yale University Press, 302 Temple Street, New Haven, CT 06520.

ONE BOOK/FIVE WAYS—William Kaufmann Inc., One First Street, Los Altos, CA 94022.

PUBLICATION DESIGN—Allen Hurlburt. Van Nostrand Reinhold Company, 135 West 50th Street, New York, N.Y. 10020.

Typography

ART OF TYPOGRAPHY, THE—Martin Solomon. Watson-Guptill Publications, 1515 Broadway, New York, N.Y. 10036.

BETTER TYPE—Betty Binns. Watson-Guptill Publications, 1515 Broadway, New York, N.Y. 10036.

DESIGNER'S GUIDE TO TEXT TYPE, THE—Jean Callan King and Tony Esposito. Van Nostrand Reinhold Company, 135 West 50th Street, New York, N.Y. 10020.

DESIGNING WITH TYPE—James Craig. Watson-Guptill Publications, 1515 Broadway, New York, N.Y. 10036.

HOW TO SPEC TYPE—Alex White. Watson-Guptill Publications, 1515 Broadway, New York, N.Y. 10036.

LETTERS—James Hutchinson. Van Nostrand Reinhold Company, 135 West 50th Street, New York, N.Y. 10020.

TIPS ON TYPE—Bill Gray. Van Nostrand Reinhold Company, 135 West 50th Street, New York, N.Y. 10020.

TYPE—David Gates. Watson-Guptill Publications, 1515 Broadway, New York, N.Y. 10036.

TYPENCYCLOPEDIA, THE—Frank J. Romano. R.R. Bowker, 245 West 17th Street, New York, N.Y. 10011.

Book production

BOOKMAKING: THE ILLUSTRATED GUIDE TO DESIGN AND PRODUCTION—Marshall Lee. R.R. Bowker, 245 West 17th Street, New York, N.Y. 10011.

BOOKS: FROM WRITER TO READER—Howard Greenfeld. Crown Publishers Inc., One Park Avenue, New York, N.Y. 10016.

DIRECTORY OF BOOK, CATALOG, AND MAGAZINE PRINTERS—John Kremer. Ad-Lib Publications, 51 N. Fifth Street, P.O. Box 1102, Fairfield, IA 52556-1102.

GETTING IT PRINTED—Mark Beach, Steve Shepro, and Ken Russon. Coast to Coast Books, 2934 Northeast 16th Avenue, Portland, OR 97212.

HOW TO PLAN PRINTING—S.D. Warren Company, 225 Franklin Street, Boston, MA 02101.

PAPER PERMANENCE: PRESERVING THE WRITTEN WORD—S.D. Warren Company, 225 Franklin Street, Boston, MA 02101.

POCKET PAL: A GRAPHIC ARTS PRODUCTION HANDBOOK—International Paper Company, 77 West 45th Street, New York, N.Y. 10036.

PRINT PRODUCTION HANDBOOK, THE—David Bann. North Light, 9933 Alliance Road, Cincinnati, OH 45242.

Desktop Publishing:

ART OF DESKTOP PUBLISHING, THE—Tony Bove, Cheryl Rhodes, and Wes Thomas. Bantam Computer Books, 666 Fifth Avenue, New York, N.Y. 10103.

DESIGN FOR DESKTOP PUBLISHING—John Miles. Chronicle Books, 1 Hallidie Plaza, San Francisco, CA 94102.

DESIGN PRINCIPLES FOR DESKTOP PUBLISHERS—Tom Lichty. Scott, Foresman Computer Books, 1900 East Lake Avenue, Glenview, IL 60025.

DESKTOP PUBLISHING: THE AWFUL TRUTH—Jeffery R. Parnau. Parnau Graphics Inc., P.O. Box 244, 2857 S. 160th Street, New Berlin, WI 53151.

GRAPHIC DESIGN FOR THE ELECTRONIC AGE—Jan V. White. Watson-Guptill Publications, 1515 Broadway, New York, N.Y. 10036.

GRID BOOK: A GUIDE TO PAGE PLANNING—Jan V. White. Letraset, 40 Eisenhower Drive, Paramus, N.J. 07653.

LOOKING GOOD IN PRINT—Roger C. Parker. Ventana Press Inc., P.O. Box 2468, Chapel Hill, N.C. 27515.

PUBLISHING FROM THE DESKTOP—John Seybold and Fritz Dressler. Bantam Computer Books, 666 Fifth Avenue, New York, N.Y. 10103.

Publishing and marketing

COMPLETE GUIDE TO SELF-PUBLISHING, THE—Tom and Marilyn Ross. Communication Creativity, P.O. Box 909, Buena Vista, CO 81211.

MARKETING YOUR BOOKS: A COLECTION OF PROFIT-MAKING IDEAS FOR AUTHORS AND PUBLISHERS—Tom and Marilyn Ross. Communication Creativity, P.O. Box 909, Buena Vista, CO 81211.

SELF-PUBLISHING MANUAL, THE—Dan Poynter. Para Publishing, P.O. Box 4232, Santa Barbara, CA 93140-4232.

1001 WAYS TO MARKET YOUR BOOK—John Kremer. Ad-Lib Publications, 51 N. Fifth Street, P.O. Box 1102, Fairfield, IA 52556-1102.

General reference

AUTHOR LAW & STRATEGIES—Brad Bunnin and Peter Beren. Nolo Press, 950 Parker Street, Berkeley, CA 94710.

CHICAGO GUIDE TO PREPARING ELECTRONIC MANUSCRIPTS—The University of Chicago Press, Chicago, IL 60637.

CHICAGO MANUAL OF STYLE, THE—The University of Chicago Press, Chicago, IL 60637.

A selected bibliography

Chicago Guide to Preparing Electronic Manuscripts. The University of Chicago Press, Chicago, IL. 1987

The Chicago Manual of Style. (13th edition) The University of Chicago Press, Chicago, IL. 1982

How to Plan Printing. S.D. Warren Company, Boston, MA. 1978

The New York Times Manual of Style and Usage. Times Books, New York, N.Y. 1976

One Book/Five Ways. William Kaufmann Inc., Los Altos, CA. 1978

Paper Permanence: Preserving the Written Word. S.D. Warren Company, Boston, MA. 1981

Pocket Pal: A Graphic Arts Production Handbook. International Paper Company, New York, N.Y. 1983

Balkin, Richard. *A Writer's Guide to Book Publishing.* Hawthorn Books Inc., New York, N.Y. 1977

Bann, David. *The Print Production Handbook.* North Light, Cincinnati, OH. 1985

Beach, Mark; Shepro, Steve; Russon, Ken. *Getting It Printed.* Coast to Coast Books, Portland, OR. 1986

Binns, Betty. *Better Type.* Watson-Guptill Publications, New York, N.Y. 1989

Blyden, Vincent. *Book Design and Manufacture.* Graphic Arts Technical Foundation, Pittsburgh, PA. 1987

Bove, Tony; Rhodes, Cheryl; Thomas, Wes. *The Art of Desktop Publishing.* Bantam Computer Books, New York, N.Y. 1986

Bunnin, Brad; Beren, Peter. *Author Law & Strategies.* Nolo Press, Berkeley, CA. 1983

Craig, James. *Designing with type.* Watson-Guptill Publications, New York, N.Y. 1980

Crane, Walter. *Of the Decorative Illustration of Books Old and New.* First published 1896. Reprinted by Bracken Books, London. 1984

Dalley, Terence. (editor) *The Complete Guide to Illustration and Design Techniques and Materials.* Chartwell Books Inc., Secaucus, N.J. 1982

Donaldson, Gerald. *Books.* Van Nostrand Reinhold Company, New York, N.Y. 1981

Gates, David. *type.* Watson-Guptill Publications, New York, N.Y. 1973

Gill, Eric. *An Essay on Typography.* First published 1931. Reprinted by David R. Godine, Boston, MA. 1988

Gray, Bill. *Tips on Type.* Van Nostrand Reinhold Co., New York, N.Y. 1983

Greenfeld, Howard. *Books: From Writer to Reader.* Crown Publishers Inc., New York, N.Y. 1976

Henderson, Bill. (editor) *The Publish-It-Yourself Handbook.* The Pushcart Book Press, Yonkers, N.Y. 1973

Holt, Robert Lawrence. *How to Publish, Promote and Sell Your Own Book.* St. Martin's Press, New York, N.Y.

Hurlburt, Allen. *Publication Design.* Van Nostrand Reinhold Company, New York, N.Y. 1976

———. *Layout: The design of the printed page.* Watson-Guptill Publications, New York, N.Y. 1977

———. *The Grid.* Van Nostrand Reinhold Company, New York, N.Y. 1978

Hutchinson, James. *Letters.* Van Nostrand Reinhold Company, New York, N.Y. 1983

King, Jean Callan; Esposito, Tony. *The Designer's Guide to Text Type.* Van Nostrand Reinhold Company, New York, N.Y. 1980

Kremer, John. *1001 Ways to Market Your Book.* Ad-Lib Publications, Fairfield, IA. 1986

——. *Directory of Book, Catalog, and Magazine Printers.* Ad-Lib Publications, Fairfield, IA. 1988

Laing, John. *Do-It-Yourself Graphic Design.* Macmillan Publishing Company, New York, N.Y. 1984

Lee, Marshall. *Bookmaking: The illustrated guide to design & production.* R.R. Bowker Company, New York, N.Y. 1979

Lewis, John. *The 20th Century Book: Its illustrations and design.* Van Nostrand Reinhold Company, New York, N.Y. 1967

Lichty, Tom. *Design Principles for Desktop Publishers.* Scott, Foresman Computer Books, Glenview, IL. 1989

Makuta, Daniel J; Lawrence, William F. *The Complete Desktop Publisher.* Compute! Publications, Inc., Greensboro, N.C. 1986

McLean, Ruari. *Modern Book Design.* Faber & Faber, London, England. 1958

Miles, John. *Design for Desktop Publishing.* Chronicle Books, San Francisco, CA. 1987

Orcutt, William Dana. *In Quest of the Perfect Book.* First published 1926. Reprinted by Books for Libraries Press, Freeport, N.Y. 1970

Parker, Roger C. *Looking Good in Print.* Ventana Press, Chapel Hill, N.C. 1988

Parnau, Jeffery R. *Desktop Publishing: The Awful Truth.* Parnau Graphics, New Berlin, WI. 1989

Poynter, Dan. *The Self-Publishing Manual.* Para Publishing, Santa Barbara, CA. Revised 1989

Romano, Frank J. *The TypEncyclopedia.* R.R. Bowker, New York, N.Y. 1984

Ross, Tom and Marilyn. *The Complete Guide to Self Publishing.* Communication Creativity, Buena Vista, CO. Revised 1989.

——. *Marketing Your Books: A Collection of Profit-Making Ideas for Authors and Publishers.* Communication Creativity, Buena Vista, CO. 1990.

Salter, Stefan. *From Cover to Cover: The occasional papers of a book designer.* Prentice Hall Inc., New York, N.Y. 1969

Seybold, John; Dressler, Fritz. *Publishing From The Desktop.* Bantam Computer Books, New York, N.Y. 1987

Solomon, Martin. *The Art of Typography.* Watson-Guptill Publications, New York, N.Y. 1986

Strunk, William; White, E.B. *The Elements of Style.* Macmillan Publishing, New York, N.Y. 1979

Swann, Alan. *How to Understand and Use Design and Layout.* North Light Books, Cincinnati, OH. 1987

Thomas, Alan G. *Fine Books.* G.P. Putnam's Sons, New York, N.Y. 1967

Tschichold, Jan. *Treasury of Alphabets and Lettering.* Omega Books Ltd., Ware, Hertfordshire, England. 1985

White, Alex. *How to Spec Type.* Watson-Guptill Publications, New York, N.Y. 1987

White, Jan V. *Editing by design.* R.R. Bowker Company, New York, N.Y. 1982

——. *Graphic Design for the Electronic Age.* Watson-Guptill Publications, New York, N.Y. 1988

——. *The Grid Book: A Guide to Page Planning.* Letraset, Paramus, N.J. 1987

Williamson, Hugh. *Methods of Book Design.* Yale University Press, New Haven, CT. 1983

Wills, F. H. *Fundamentals of Layout.* First published 1965. Reprinted by Dover Publications Inc., New York, N.Y. 1971

Wilson, Adrian. *The Design of Books.* Peregrine Smith Books, Layton, UT. 1974

Wilson, Robert A. *Modern Book Collecting.* Alfred A. Knopf, New York, N.Y. 1980

Glossary

*Most of the words listed in this glossary have more than one definition; only those pertaining to the topic of this book are included. Words set in **bold type** in the definitions are explained elsewhere in the glossary.*

A

AA. Author's Alteration. A mark used when checking proofs from the typesetter, indicating that the alteration (or, correction) is the author's rather than the typesetter's. As opposed to TE — Typographical Error.

acid-free papers. One of the components used in manufacturing paper since the 1870s contains an acid which, over time, causes book pages to become brittle and disintegrate. In response to demands from the Library of Congress and numerous groups of other concerned people, manufacturers are now changing their methods and are producing papers that meet certain levels of pH and alkaline reserve. Under normal conditions, these papers — which are acid-free — can last 300 years or more. *See also* **pH.**

advertisement card. A list of other books by the same author, usually appearing on a page of its own as part of the front matter or the back matter.

album. Term used by traditional typographers to describe books or pages that are horizontal in shape. The same format is now better known as *landscape* or *horizontal.*

aligning numerals. Numerals designed to be the same height as the capital letters of a typeface. ABC123456DEF. Also called **modern numerals.** As opposed to **non-aligning numerals,** which have ascenders and descenders similar to lowercase letters — abc123456def.

arabic numerals. 1, 2, 3, 4, 5, etc., as opposed to **roman numerals** — i, ii, iii, iv, v, etc. *See also* **roman numerals.**

alphabet length. The length of the complete lowercase alphabet (a-z) of a typeface when set normally (that is, without any adjusting of letter spacing). This will vary from one typeface to another, depending on the width of individual letters. The alphabet length is used during the **copyfitting** process.

ascenders. The strokes and loops that extend upward from the body of lowercase letters b, d, f, h, k, l, and t. As opposed to **descenders** — the strokes and loops that drop down from the body of lowercase letters g, j, p, q, and y.

B

back matter. The section of a book following the main text. Can include notes, appendices, bibliography, glossary, index, etc.

bar code. A symbol consisting of thick and thin lines encoded with information now required when marketing a product. Books require a specific bar code called **Bookland EAN.** When a scanner is wiped across the lines it relays to a computer the book's ISBN and price. Bookland is a numeric code used throughout the world to identify books. EAN stands for European Article Number, although the number is now used beyond the boundaries of Europe.

baseline. The invisible line on which the body of type sits. One way of determining the size of a typeface is to measure the distance from one baseline to another.

basis weight. The weight in pounds of one ream (500 sheets) of paper. Each category of paper has its own standard size. Papers used for the pages of a book are usually 25" x 38". Papers used for covers and dust jackets are usually 20" x 26". *See also* **grammage.**

bastard title page. A page that contains only the title of a book; often the first printed page in a book. At one time books were printed and sold without covers, and buyers would get them bound in a style appropriate for their own libraries. The book's title would be printed on this first page as a means of identifying the stack of unbound pages; it also acted as protection for the legitimate title page, which appeared as the third page. Often the bastard title page was not bound with the book.

bibliography. A list of books relating to a specific topic, period, or writer. The bibliography seen at the back of most books identifies the sources used in the author's research.

blank leaf. The first page of a hardcover book — the one attached to the **endpaper,** which is the sheet that holds the pages to the cover boards. Traditionally, this page was kept blank.

bleeding. The action of "running off the page," as in the case of a photograph that extends to the very edge of a page. For a photograph to bleed, it has to be printed approximately $\frac{1}{16}$" beyond the page and then trimmed. It can bleed off one edge, or two, or three, or all four. When it bleeds off all four edges it is called a *full bleed.*

blind folio. A page number is called a **folio.** When a page number does not appear on a page it is said to be a blind folio.

blueline, or **blues.** A set of proofs made by a printer immediately before running the presses,

to check that everything is as it should be — pages are aligned, captions and illustrations are in correct positions, etc. These proofs are usually printed in a pale blue ink on a specially coated paper. *See also* **proof**; **check copy.**

blurb. A brief notice about the book or its author, usually found on the back of a book, or on the inside flaps of the dust jacket.

boards. *See* **mechanicals.**

Bookland EAN. *See* **bar code.**

book paper. Paper used for printing books. Also referred to as **text paper.**

bond paper. Paper used for printing letterheads, business forms, leaflets, etc.

bulk. The thickness of paper, usually rated in PPI (pages per inch).

bullet. A dot used for either ornamentation or emphasis. It can be closed (•) or open (○). As a rule, bullets should not be larger than the **x-height** of the accompanying text. If smaller, then they should be centered on the x-height. A *bulleted item* is one that is highlighted with a bullet**.**

C

camera-ready. When all the blocks of type, halftones, etc. are in their correct position and ready to be photographed by the printer, they are said to be camera-ready.

C1S. Coated 1 Side. Refers to certain papers (such as those used for covers and dust jackets) that have been coated on one side only.

caption. Defined variously as the heading above a picture and as the descriptive passage beneath it. In this book the word is used to mean the descriptive passage beneath a picture. *See also* **legend.**

cap height. A method of defining the size of a specific typeface by measuring the height of its capital letters. As opposed to measuring the body of lowercase letters — known as **x-height.**

case bound. A hardcover book. Also referred to as *cloth bound.*

cast-off. The process of determining how many pages will be required to accommodate a specific amount of text once it has been set in type. *See also* **copyfitting.**

chapter head. The number of a chapter.

chapter opener. The page on which a chapter begins.

character. Each letter, number, punctuation mark, and symbol in a line of text is called a character.

character count. To determine the length of a manuscript, or of any other piece of text, you must count the number of characters as well as the number of spaces between words. This is called a character count.

character set. A recently coined term for the specific assortment of characters available in a particular typeface.

characters per pica (CPP). The number of characters of a specific size and style of typeface that will fit into a 1-pica space. Most type style books will include a CPP table which you can use to determine how many characters will fit in a pica and, subsequently, how many characters will fit on a page of type.

check copy. When the pages of a book have been printed, and before they are bound, printers check them carefully one more time to make sure they are all correctly positioned. At this stage they are referred to as a check copy, or an **F&G** — Folded and Gathered.

CIP. Cataloging In Publication — a program enabling publishers to print in their books library catalog information that has been pre-assigned by the Library of Congress. This information should be placed on the reverse of the title page.

coated paper. Paper that has been coated with clay or enamel. Without this coating a paper will absorb more ink, sometimes causing text and photographs to appear muddy and out of focus.

Although most people associate "coated" with "high-gloss," there are also matte-coated papers — ones that have a dull surface. Matte-coated papers are suitable when cost is a consideration, and when you have only a few black and white photographs.

colophon. Originally this was the trademark of a publisher-printer, and it always appeared as the last item in a book. Today it usually lists the people who helped produce the book, and sometimes it includes details about the paper and the typefaces that were used. There is a tendency now to print it on the copyright page, although some publishers still put it on the last page, if they use it at all.

color (of type). The grayness of a page of text as created by the combination of various weights (thicknesses) of type and their relationship to the surrounding white gaps. This is a major criterion in judging a book's appearance. The more uniform it is, the more comfortable it will be to the eye.

color separation. The process of breaking down a color image into four sheets of film (yellow, magenta, cyan, and black). When these separate images are printed on paper they combine to create a full range of colors. Today this process is being done by computerized scanners.

comb binding. The method of book binding in which the pages are trimmed on all four sides and punched with holes on one side, then threaded into a plastic comb-like clamp.

condensed type. A typeface that has been made narrower, either by the original designer or by a computer typesetting system. As opposed to **expanded type.** Condensed types are used when you have a limited space in which to fit a lot of text.

continuous tone. A photograph is a continous tone image: The tones range from black to white, with a wide spectrum of grays in between. As opposed to a **line drawing** which consists only of black and white. *See also* **halftone.**

copyedit. To edit a piece of *copy* (e.g., a manuscript) before it is set in type. Not to be confused with *proofread* which refers specifically to the checking of typeset proofs. *See also* **proof**; **proofreader's marks.**

copyfitting. The process of either (1) fitting the text, illustrations, etc., into a given number of pages, or (2) determining how many pages will be needed to fit a given amount of text, illustrations, etc. A number of variables will be taken into consideration, such as size and style of typeface, width and depth of text columns, overall size of pages, etc.

CPP. *See* **characters per pica.**

cover stock. Paper used for covers of paperbacks, or for dust jackets of hardcovers. It is slightly thicker than paper used for book pages.

cropping. Blocking off extraneous areas of a photograph or illustration to create a stronger image. You should either mark the white borders where you want to crop or cover the image with a piece of tracing paper on which you indicate the area to be printed.

D

descenders. The strokes and loops that drop down from the body of lowercase letters g, j, p, q, and y. As opposed to **ascenders** — the strokes and loops that extend upward from the body of lowercase letters b, d, f, h, k, l, and t.

DICODOB. An acronym for a question: Does It Complement Overall Design of Book? I coined the word to remind myself when trying new ideas that all elements of a book's design must work together if the overall design is to be one of total harmony.

dingbat. A piece of ornamental type.

diphthong. A combination of two letters, as in æ and œ, that represent a specific vowel sound. Diphthongs are rarely printed today, and most words that once required them have changed their spelling. For example: "encyclopedia" ("encyclopædia") and "ecology" ("œcology"). *See also* **ligature.**

display initial. The generic term for a large letter used at the beginning of a chapter or paragraph. A **drop initial** (or, *sunken initial*) is one that drops down into the text. A **raised initial** (or, *stick-up initial*) is one that stands on the baseline of the first line of text and rises into the white space above it.

display type. The large type used for titles, headings, and subheadings is called display type. Generally it is 18-point type or larger. As opposed to **text type**, which is used for the main body of text.

drop folio. A folio is a page number. When it appears at the bottom of a page it is referred to as a drop folio.

drop initial. *See* **display initial.**

dummy. (1) A rough, miniature replica of a book indicating what will be on each page. The more complicated the book's design and layout, the more complete should the dummy be, because only then can you be sure that everything will fit where you want it to. (2) The word can also be used as a verb, as when a person will "dummy up a page" — will paste individual pieces of text on pages to see how they fit. (3) A book of blank pages cut and folded to your specifications, as a sample of how your book will look if printed on a specific grade of paper. This can sometimes be obtained from either the printer or a paper supplier.

duotone. A **halftone** that is printed in two colors — usually blue and black, brown and black, or gray and black — using two separate negatives. The resulting image has more depth than a regular halftone.

dust jacket. The paper cover of a **case bound** book. Originally it was intended to protect the cloth used on a book's cover. Now it is used mainly as an advertising tool in selling the book.

E

EAN. *See* **bar code.**

em. A unit of measure which will vary with each typeface because it is based on the size of a capital letter M. In a 10-point type the em measures 10 points x 10 points. In a 12-point type the em measures 12 points x 12 points. Etc. The em measure is normally used to identify spacing within a line of type as in the case of a paragraph indent, which may be 1 em or 2 em. *See also* **en.**

em dash. A punctuation mark used to indicate a break in a thought or in the structure of a sentence. It can also be used to indicate missing material in a sentence. You have the choice of leaving or not leaving a space before and after an em dash. *See also* **en dash.**

en. A unit of measure that is half the width of an **em.** In a 10-point type the en measures 5 points x 10 points. In a 12-point type the en measures 6 points x 12 points. Etc. The en measure is normally used to separate words. It is sometimes called a *nut* to avoid confusing the spoken words "en" and "em." *See also* **em.**

en dash. A punctuation mark that is wider than a hyphen, but half the width of an **em dash.** It is used to link two inclusive elements, such as dates (1970–75), pages (142–56), etc. *See also* **em dash.**

endpaper. The thick sheet of paper that holds the pages to the boards of a hardcover book. One half is glued entirely against the cover and the other half is attached to the first page of the book by a thin strip of glue. A hardcover book has two endpapers — one at the front and one at the back. Paperbacks do not have endpapers. Also called *end leaves.*

epilogue. A summary, or the concluding remarks, of a play or literary work. As opposed to **prologue**, which is an introduction to a work. These terms are rarely used in books today, but when they are they can be spelled also without the final *ue* — epilog, prolog.

errata slip. A slip of paper inserted in a book to correct errors that were not spotted before the book was printed. The Latin word *errata* refers to two or more errors, while *erratum* indicates only one error.

expanded type. A typeface that has been expanded, either by the original designer or by a computer typesetting system. As opposed to **condensed type** which has been made narrower. Expanded types are used mainly in headings or in small blocks of text and are not suitable for normal body text.

extract. A citation, or excerpt, that is printed as a separate paragraph because it is considered too long to include within the normal text. Usually the paragraph is indented and set in a type size smaller than the rest of the body text.

F

F&G. *See* **check copy.**

family of type. Each typeface comes in a family that includes several different styles such as roman, italic, bold, semi-bold, etc. One example of a family would be Bookman Light, Bookman Light Italic, Bookman Medium, Bookman Medium Italic, Bookman Demibold, Bookman Demibold Italic, Bookman Bold, Bookman Bold Italic.

film lamination. A thin, clear sheet of protective film that can be applied to a book cover or jacket. This is probably the most popular form of protection used on books, even though in damp weather it sometimes causes covers to curl. Its hard, glossy surface enhances colors and is difficult to tear.

flush. Text that has an unbroken edge on the left is said to be *flush left.* When all lines create an unbroken edge on the right they are called *flush right.* An illustration, or box, is considered flush if its outer edges touch a border or are aligned with a block of text. *See also* **justified type.**

folio. A page number.

font. A set of characters (letters, numbers, punctuation, etc.) of a specific size within a typeface. A group of 10-point Baskerville characters is one font, while a group of 12-point Baskerville characters is another font. Today, the word is sometimes used interchangeably with **typeface**, although this can lead to confusion.

footers. *See* **running heads.**

foreword. A piece written by someone other than the book's author and appearing as the first text item in the front matter. This writer is usually a famous personality and/or an authority on the topic of the book. As opposed to **preface**, which is a piece written by the book's author explaining why or how the book was written.

form. Each side of the large sheet of paper on which the pages of a book are printed is called a form. *See also* **signature.**

front matter. The section of a book preceding the main text. Included are the title page, foreword, preface, introduction, table of contents, etc. Sometimes called *preliminaries* or *prelims*.

frontispiece. Originally, a frontispiece was an illustration facing the title page; today the term is used to define the page itself rather than what is on it. In many book designs, titles and illustrations stretch across both pages.

G

galley. The first proof copy of text after it has been set in type. This is used by the **proofreader** to check for errors in typesetting. A galley can also be called a **proof.** In earlier days hand-set type was stored in long metal trays called *galleys*. When a proof was needed, ink was rolled onto the type while it was still in the galley, and a piece of paper was then pressed down onto it.

glossary. A list of definitions of technical or special words used in a particular book or treatise.

grain. The direction in which the fibers flow within a piece of paper, as determined by the method of manufacture. In a paper that is *grain long* the fibers run along the length of the sheet, and in a *grain short* paper they run across the sheet. The direction of grain will affect the way a paper folds.

grammage. The metric method of determining the **basis weight** of paper. This method is used in most countries outside the United States and is based on the number of grams per square meter. *See also* **basis weight.**

greek type. An unintelligible mixture of letters formed into non-words and used by designers and graphic artists to substitute for actual text — which may not yet be written — so they can get an idea of how the layout will look.

grid. A system of vertical and horizontal lines used to apply principles of proportion and their relationship to each other in a design layout. It enables you to organize your pages so they all have a sense of uniformity. Ideally, it should act as a guide only and should not be allowed to constrict a design.

gutter. (1) A gap between two columns of text. (2) The trench in the center of a two-page spread, created by the binding of the book. *See also* **gutter margin.**

gutter margin. The margin closest to the binding.

H

hairline. The thinnest of **rules** (straight lines) — only ¼ point thick.

halftone. A photograph after it has been rephotographed through a fine mesh screen and prepared for printing on the page of a book, newspaper, magazine, etc. The mesh screen breaks down the image into dots of various sizes which, when printed, give the illusion of shades of gray. *See also* **continuous tone.**

half title page. A page on which only the section title, or the book's title, appears.

hanging indentation. With hanging indentation the first line of a paragraph of text begins flush against the left-hand edge of the **text area** and the rest of the paragraph is indented. This glossary is set with hanging indentation.

hanging punctuation. When certain punctuation marks appear at the end of justified lines of type they create tiny gaps in an otherwise evenly aligned vertical edge. To avoid this, many printers will *hang* the offending mark in the margin, even if they have to set it in a smaller point size to make it less obvious.

headbands. Strips of colored thread that can be seen at the top and bottom of a hardcover's spine. These strengthen the back of the book and act as protection when people tug at the top of the spine to pull a book from a tightly packed shelf.

headers. *See* **running heads.**

house papers. The papers a printer keeps in inventory. Since **stock** is used as a synonym for "paper," the term "house paper" is less likely to cause confusion.

I

image area. The area within a page's margins. It encompasses not only the **text area** but also the areas occupied by illustrations, graphs, tables, headings, etc. Also called *live area.*

imposition. The sequence in which pages are laid on a **signature** so that they appear in correct numerical order when the signature is printed and folded.

imprint. The name under which a publisher publishes a book. For example, *Londonborn Publications* is the imprint under which this book is published. Some publishers use different imprints to produce very specific categories of books.

introduction. The introduction *introduces* the book's topic and sometimes updates the material that appears in the main part of the book. It appears as the last piece of text in the front matter. *See also* **foreword; preface.**

ISBN. International Standard Book Number. A ten-digit number used to identify the country or language of the publisher, the publisher's name, and the book's title. It should appear on the reverse of the title page, and on the back cover; also, when possible, on the spine and on the inside flap of the dust jacket.

italic type. The slanting type used most often for emphasis. It was originally designed to save space. As opposed to **roman type**, which is what you are reading now.

J

justified type. Type that has been set with all lines of equal length. To achieve this, the spacing between words and letters has been adjusted (made wider or narrower). As opposed to **ragged** type, which is what you are reading now.

K

kerning. Adjusting the space between two specific letters which, because of their shape, appear to be too far apart or, in some cases, too close together. As in WA (WA) and ND (ND).

keyline. (1) A thin outline or box denoting the position of a piece of artwork. (2) Artwork in the final stage of preparation for printing.

L

landscape. A horizontal format for a book, illustration, etc. As opposed to **portrait**, which is a vertical format for a book, illustration, etc. These two shapes are also called *horizontal* and *vertical* respectively.

leaders. A row of dots, used as a guide when connecting two elements such as in tables of contents or in tabular work.

LCCN. Library of Congress Catalog Number.

leading. The spacing between lines. Originally, this was created by placing strips of lead between individual lines of metal type. Also referred to as **line spacing.**

legend. (1) A list of symbols and their definitions, usually found beneath a map or chart. (2) A descriptive passage beneath an illustration. This is more frequently called a **caption.**

legibility. The ease with which letterforms, or words, can be recognized. This is influenced by the size of a typeface combined with the length of the line of type and the amount of spacing between the words and between individual letters. In making all these decisions you must consider how legible the type will be when it appears on the page. *See also* **readability.**

ligature. Two or more letters that are joined together to conserve space. Most common ligatures are ff, fi, fl, ffi, ffl. *See also* **diphthong.**

lightbox. A box with a light in it. A device used when pasting pieces of text onto **mechanicals.** The light showing through the paper will make it easier for you to align the pieces.

line drawing. A drawing in which there are no grays or middle tones, and which can be reproduced without conversion to a **halftone.**

line length. *See* **measure.**

line spacing. *See* **leading.**

lining numerals. *See* **aligning numerals.**

live area. *See* **image area.**

locator. A point of reference used to direct a reader from an item in an index to the relevant passage in the book. Usually this is a page number, although it can also be a section number, or paragraph number, as can be seen in *The Chicago Manual of Style.*

lowercase. Small letters, as opposed to **uppercase.** In the days of hand-set type the individual pieces of type were stored in wooden trays (called *cases*), each of which was divided into a myriad of sections. The capital letters were stored in one case, and the smaller letters were stored in another. When being used, these cases were placed one above the other in front of the typesetter — the upper case containing the capitals and the lower case the small letters. When printers moved across the country to California they rearranged the cases so that all letters, large and small, could fit in one. This became known as the *California Job Case.*

M

Manufacturing Clause. A clause in the old Copyright Act which required publishers to print a notice in each book stating exactly where the book was manufactured. The clause expired on July 1, 1986.

matte finish. A non-shiny coating applied to the surface of a paper.

measure. Typesetters refer to the length of a line of type as a measure, and they define it in **picas.** Also known as *line length.*

mechanical binding. A book binding method that uses plastic combs or wire spirals.

mechanicals. Boards on which all the pieces of text and artwork have been pasted in preparation for printing.

minus leading. A method of reducing leading rather than adding it. As in the case of 10/9½, in which a 10 point type is placed on a minus ½ point leading. This can be done only with typefaces that have short **x-height,** and would have been impossible in days of metal type. *See also* **vertical justification.**

mirror image. When the basic layout of a left-hand page is the exact opposite of the layout on the right-hand page it is said to be a mirror image.

modern numerals. *See* **non-aligning numerals.**

monospacing. When all letters of the alphabet are of equal width they are considered monospaced. For example, in the basic Courier typewriter face an *i* takes up the same amount of room as does an *m.* As opposed to **proportional spacing,** in which each letter occupies a space proportionate to its width.

N

neutral pH paper. *See* **acid-free papers.**

new edition. A reprinting of a book with new information added. Not to be confused with *new printing,* which is a reprinting without any changes other than perhaps correction of typographical errors. A new edition requires a new ISBN, but a new printing does not.

new printing. *See* **new edition.**

non-aligning numerals. Numerals designed with ascenders and descenders similar to lowercase letters. abc123456def. Also called *old style numerals*. As opposed to **aligning numerals**, which are designed to be the same height as capital letters — ABC123456DEF.

notch binding. A method of book binding. Only three edges of the pages are trimmed, and the fourth (the spine edge) is cut with diagonal notches. Glue is inserted into the notches, to gain a firm grip on the pages.

nut. *See* **en.**

O

old-style numerals. *See* **non-aligning numerals.**

opacity. The degree to which a particular paper will permit print to **show through** from one side to the other. As a general rule, light-weight uncoated papers (50-lb, 55-lb, etc.) will be less opaque than heavy coated ones and are therefore more likely to permit show through.

opaquing. The process of blocking out unwanted marks or areas on a negative so they will not print. Similarly, a white opaque can be used to cover an unwanted mark or area on a white page.

orphan. When the first line of an indented paragraph is left at the bottom of a page while the remainder of the paragraph moves to the next page it is called an orphan. This word is sometimes used interchangeably — and incorrectly — with the word *widow*. *See also* **widow.**

P

page proof. *See* **proof.**

pallet. A wooden platform which can be raised and moved by a fork-lift. Cartons of books are usually shipped to the publisher from the printer on pallets.

part title. The title of a section of a book. It usually appears by itself on a right-hand page.

PE. Printer's Error. When correcting early proofs you should write "PE" alongside errors made by the typesetter because these will be corrected without charge. However, you will have to pay for author's alterations (AA). The term "PE" dates back to days when typesetters worked for printing companies. More accurately, the term now should be TE (Typesetter's Error).

perfect binding. The method of book binding in which all four edges of the pages are cut off and the spine is glued to the cover.

pH. A symbol used to express the acidity or alkalinity of a solution or material. On a scale of 0 to 14 the neutral point is 7. Numbers less than 7 indicate an acid nature, while numbers greater than 7 indicate an alkaline nature. *See also* **acid-free papers.**

photostat. An inexpensive photocopy of a **halftone**, illustration, or typeset copy. Commonly referred to as a *stat*. *See also* **PMT; Velox.**

pica. A unit of measure used to determine the length of a line of type, or the width of an area on a page. Traditionally, 1 pica = .166", which means that 6 picas measure slightly less than 1" (.996"). However, some computer programs have opted to round it out to an even 6 picas per inch.

PMS. Pantone Matching System. A standard set of colors used in the graphic arts and printing industries and generally referred to by numbers, as in PMS 15 (a particular shade of orange).

PMT. Photomechanical Transfer. An inexpensively produced screened print made on photographic paper. Its quality is slightly better than that of a **photostat**, yet not as fine as that of a **Velox.**

point. A unit of measurement used to determine the height of a typeface and/or its **leading**. Also used to determine the thickness of a **rule** (straight line). 12 points = 1 pica. 72 points = 1".

portrait. A vertical format for a book, illustration, etc. As opposed to **landscape**, which is a horizontal format for a book, illustration, etc. These two shapes are also called *vertical* and *horizontal* respectively.

position stat. A **photostat** used on a **mechanical** to indicate which picture is to be positioned in that particular position and how it is to be cropped. *See also* **cropping.**

PPB. Paper, Printing, and Binding. In planning a book most publishers estimate all possible costs in order to determine how much they will have to charge for it in order to make a profit. Because the three major areas of expense are usually paper, printing and binding this estimating process is sometimes referred to as PPB.

PPI. Pages Per Inch. In order to figure the thickness of a book you will need to know the PPI of the paper you are using. This is determined by the **bulk** of the paper.

preface. A part of the front matter written by the author and explaining why and how the book was written. As opposed to **foreword**, which is usually written by someone other than the author.

preliminaries (prelims). *See* **front matter.**

prologue. An introduction to a book, usually placed in the front matter. As opposed to **epilogue**, which is the summary or concluding remarks of a play or literary work, and which is usually placed in the back matter. These terms are rarely used in books today, but when they are they can be spelled also without the final *ue* — prolog, epilog.

proof. A preliminary printing of text that is used to check for errors made by the typesetter. When the errors have been corrected, a *revised proof* is made and checked to ensure that all corrections were made and that no other errors occurred in the process. *Page proofs* are proofs of entire pages that can be checked for accuracy of line breaks, page breaks, **widows**, etc. *See also* **galley**; **blueline.**

proofreader. A person who reads **proofs** looking for errors.

proofreader's marks. A series of abbreviations and symbols used by **proofreaders** when checking a **proof** for errors. The same marks are used by copy editors when they **copyedit** a manuscript before it is set in type.

proportional spacing. When all letters of the alphabet occupy a space in proportion to their individual shape and size. As opposed to **monospacing**, in which they all occupy the same width — an *i* being the same width as an *m,* for example.

Q

quad. In hand-set type a quad is a piece of metal used to create space between words. The word is an abbreviation of *quadrate* — "an approximately square or cubical area, space, or body." Quads come in various widths.

R

ragged. Lines of type that are uneven in length are called ragged. If the lines are even on the left edge but uneven on the right, they are said to be "flush left, ragged right." If uneven on the left but even on the right they are "flush right, ragged left." Columns of uneven depth are also said to be ragged.

readability. The ease with which words can be read. Readability and **legibility** are the two main criteria for good typesetting. Both are influenced by the size of a typeface combined with the length of the line of type and the amount of spacing between the words and between the individual letters.

recto. Latin for "right." A right-hand page is called a recto. As opposed to a left-hand page, which is called a **verso**. One way to remember which is which: R for "right," R for "recto."

Request for Quote Form. A form sent to printers when requesting an estimate of costs to print and bind a book.

reversed type. Type is considered reversed when it is printed as white against a black or colored background.

revised proof. *See* **proof**.

river. A continuous stream of white space running down between words in a block of text. This undesirable effect is created when spaces between words appear at about the same point on successive lines. It is particularly prevalent with narrow typefaces when set **justified** in wide columns.

roman numerals. Numerals formed by using letters of the alphabet — i, ii, iii, iv, v, x, c, etc. In traditional book design these lowercase letters are used to identify the pages in the front matter, and capital letters (I, II, III, IV, V, X, C, etc.) are used to number the various sections or chapters. When books were set by hand the typesetters did not wait for the front matter pages to be written or designed. They would set the main text beginning with the arabic numeral 1 and then use the roman numerals to number the front matter pages. *See also* **arabic numerals.**

roman type. Normal, upright type such as what you are now reading. As opposed to **italic type**, which slants to one side and takes up less space.

rules. Straight lines that are identified either by their thickness in points and fractions of points or as *fine, medium,* and *thick*. The thinnest (¼ point) is called a *hairline rule*.

running heads. The lines of type that run across the top of a page, usually with the book's title or the chapter title. Also called *headers*. When these lines appear at the bottom of a page they are often referred to as *running feet,* or *footers*.

S

saddle stitching. The method of book binding in which the pages are stapled together at the spine. Usually books with fewer than 64 pages are saddle-stitched.

sans serif. A typeface that does not have *serifs* — those tiny chips at the beginning and ending of letter strokes. Also, sans serif letters do not stress, nor — with rare exceptions such as Optima — do they have thick and thin variations to their strokes.

scaling. The process of determining the proportion of an image (e.g., a photograph) in order to fit it into a specific space.

scanner. A computerized device for making **color separations**. Also, a device that can "read" a block of type, or illustration, and recreate it in a computer.

score. To make a dent in a paper or card so as to facilitate folding. This is usually done by special machines, although you can do it yourself by running the back of a knife blade carefully along the edge of a metal ruler on the paper.

serif. *See* **sans serif.**

set solid. Type that is set without **leading** between the lines is said to be set solid. A 12-point type without leading is defined as 12/12, for example.

set-width. The width of the metal block on which type sits.

show through. An image printed on one side of a page that shows through the paper and can be seen on the other side. This can be prevented by matching the two print areas back-to-back, or by using a more opaque paper.

shrink wrap. One method of protecting the covers of books when they are being shipped from the printer. A tough transparent plastic is wrapped securely around the books, either individually or in groups.

side stitching. The method of book binding in which the pages are trimmed on all four sides and bound with metal staples near the spine. If twine is used instead of metal staples the method is called *side sewing*.

signature. Pages of a book are printed on one large sheet of paper which is then folded and trimmed. Depending on the size of the original sheet, and the size of the pages, there can be either 8, 12, 16, 24, or 32 pages on each sheet. When folded and trimmed these pages are referred to as one signature. Traditionally somone would check that all pages were in the correct order before signing one to indicate approval. Each side of the original sheet is called a **form.**

sinkage. The deep gap that may appear between the top of a **text area** and the top of the first element on a page — usually a chapter title or section title.

slipcase. An open-ended box in which one or more books are sold as a unit.

small capitals. Uppercase letters designed specifically to be the same size as, or slightly larger than, the x-height of lowercase letters. ABCDEFG. Not all typefaces have small capitals.

Smyth sewing. The method of book binding in which the pages are sewn together with thread and then glued on to the cover.

spec sheet. Specifications sheet. A list specifying exactly what you want done in a particular phase of production. A spec sheet to a typesetter would indicate what typefaces you want for the various components of text, the width and depth of text columns, the amount of spacing between lines, etc. A spec sheet to a printer would indicate what paper you want, how the book is to be bound, how many copies to be printed, etc. In each case, the spec sheet is an invaluable safeguard against misunderstanding on the part of the people carrying out your instructions.

spine. The bound edge of a book, where the pages are held together.

spread. Abbreviation of *two-page spread*, or *double-page spread* — two pages seen side by side. In designing a book you should consider the two pages as one unit, not as two separate units.

stat. *See* **photostat.**

stet. A **proofreader's mark** reversing a correction — "let it stand as it was."

stick-up initial. *See* **display initial.**

stock. In the printing industry, paper is referred to as stock.

stock photos. Photographs offered by photographers or their agents for use in publications on payment of a fee.

T

TE. Typesetter's Error. *See also* **PE.**

text area. The area on a page occupied by the text. As opposed to the **image area**, which is the area encompassing all the text, illustrations, headings, etc.

text paper. The grade of paper most often used for printing books. The word "text" is an abbreviation of "texture" and does not refer to printed text.

thumbnail. A rough sketch of a page layout or design idea, usually greatly reduced yet still in proportion to the final dimensions. An abbreviation of "thumbnail sketch."

tombstone. The effect created when a subheading in one column of text aligns with a subheading in an adjoining column of text. This can be avoided by rewriting one of the subheadings and placing it earlier or later in the text.

trim size. The measurements of a page after it has been printed and trimmed. For example: 6" x 9", 7" x 10", 8½" x 11". The first figure always applies to the width (i.e., from left to right) and the second figure applies to the height.

type-high. The height of a piece of metal type, from its base to its printing surface. All metal typefaces made in the United States had a standard height of .9186", which assured that they would create an even impression on paper when laid out on a press.

typo. An error made while setting type. A typographical error.

U

ultraviolet coating (UV). An ultraviolet coating that can be applied to the printed cover of a book to protect the ink from rubbing off. It is a liquid when first applied to the cover, but it hardens and creates either a matte or glossy surface.

uppercase. Capital letters. *See also* **lowercase.**

V

Velox. An inexpensive screened print which can be pasted onto a **mechanical** and reproduced without going through the more expensive halftone negative process. Images printed from Veloxes lack the quality of those produced from halftone negatives, although they are better than those produced from PMTs. *See also* PMT; **photostat.**

verso. Latin for "that which was turned." The left-hand page of a book. As opposed to the **recto** — the right-hand page of a book.

vertical justification. The adjustment of spacing between lines of type to force a block of text to conform to a specified depth. For example, if the text on one page is a line or two shorter than the text on the facing page, you can add minute increments of **leading** throughout the text to make them even. However, purists frown on this and would prefer the irregular depth of text blocks to the non-alignment of individual lines of text across a **spread.**

W

weight (of type). A style of type, as in *regular, semi-bold, bold, condensed, italic.* Most typefaces offer a variety of weights which can be used to add variety to the design of a page without resorting to different typefaces.

widow. This word has a slightly different meaning for different people. The one generally accepted is: The last word or words of a paragraph creating a short line at the top of a page or column. A widow can also be the last line of ANY paragraph if there are only one or two words on the line. To some people a widow is the first line of a paragraph when it stands alone at the bottom of a page, although this is generally referred to as an **orphan**. The one thing most people agree on is that widows and orphans should be avoided whenever possible, whether they appear at the top or the bottom of a page or somewhere in between.

window. An opaque area on a layout which, when reproduced on negative film during the plate-making process, will leave a clear transparent space for a **halftone** to be placed.

word break. A word that is hyphenated at the end of a line of type.

X

x-height. A unit of measure used to identify the size of a typeface. It indicates the height of lowercase letters, not including their ascenders or descenders. As opposed to **cap height**, which indicates the height of uppercase letters.

Index

Book design by the author.
Editing by Jackie Pels.
Drawings and pasteup by David R. Johnson.
Typefaces: Utopia and Utopia Expert,
Adobe Systems Inc., set 11/12.
Printed and bound by Thomson-Shore, Michigan,
on 60-lb. Glatfelter Spring Forge White acid-free paper.

2847